LOW AND OUTSIDE

BY *Jerry Kettle*

WITH ED ADDEO

LOW AND

THE CONFESSIONS

OF A MINOR LEAGUER

ILLUSTRATED WITH PHOTOGRAPHS

OUTSIDE

COWARD-McCANN, INC., New York

Contents

Illustrations follow page 64

LOW AND OUTSIDE

1

Who the Hell Is Jerry Kettle?

*H*ow do you answer a telephone when your hands are full of manure? Simple. You pick up a large banana tree leaf and use it as a sort of hand antimacassar, and try to breathe through your mouth.

This happened the other day when I was working in my dad's nursery in Pasadena, California. On the other end of the line was an old friend of mine who was in town for a few days and wanted to have a few beers. We hadn't seen each other for a year or so. Anyway, I'd say yes to my worst enemy if it meant a few beers.

I met him at a local cocktail lounge, and we spent the evening talking over old times, laughing like hell at the wild and funny things we did when we were playing ball together. My friend's name is Dallas Green, and he pitches

9

for the Philadelphia Phillies. He was in town for an off day before the Phils opened a series with the L. A. Dodgers. God, we must have drunk beer and laughed like hell until two in the morning. Dallas and I were roommates for a few years when we played together for the Phillies' farm organization in the minor leagues.

The evening touched off a helluva lot of memories for me, memories almost every kid in the country would like to have.

It struck me that night, as I bid farewell again to Dallas —after getting a few free tickets, of course—that hardly anyone really knows much about what life is like in the minor leagues, so I thought I'd put down a few of these memories I mentioned.

Me? My name's Jerry Kettle, and don't bother asking the next question.

I'll tell you.

There's no sense going through a family history. A kid will play ball whether his father is Ty Cobb or Lawrence of Arabia. He'll play in parks, sandlots, his backyard, up against the wall of a warehouse, or even in the middle of a busy city street where one sewer is home plate and another is second base (a fire hydrant is first and a Chevy's front fender is third).

And if you'll stop to notice, each kid is a pitcher. Anyone *not* pitching is only playing his position until *his* chance to pitch comes. Pitching, to kids, is like being the only cop in the world. To adults, it's like being the guy who blew the bugle when Custer charged.

I was a pitcher, too. I still am, in fact, but nobody's paying me for it anymore.

The fact is, though, my father did play a little ball. He never played any pro ball, or even semi-pro. I guess his greatest achievement was getting an offer to play with the Seattle Rainiers, in the Pacific Coast League. In those days they wanted him to travel there from L. A. at his own expense, which is comparable today to offering a bum a job in Venezuela and telling him you'll meet him there.

My dad didn't have much money in those days, having just married my mother and just been released by the Army. Kind of a double-whammy, I guess. Also, he was known and liked in Pasadena, which gives a man a good sense of security. It also helps if your father owns a nursery, which my grandfather did. Anyway, Dad didn't think taking the chance was worth it, so he didn't go to Seattle.

Thus one more pitcher bit the dust.

Shortly after that, my dad played in a softball league for a few years, the only overhand league in the country. I was a little dinky guy by that time and became a bat boy. The team was Kettle's Nursery, my dad's team, so I didn't need much talent to wrangle the job. Since then, I wish I had a nickel for every time I envied the bat boy sitting on the bench while I was getting my brains knocked out. Happiness is being in the dugout while another pitcher gives up six runs.

My earliest memory of even trying to play ball was when I was bat boy for this softball team. I remember sneaking off behind the backstop to fool around with a ball and a glove while everyone shouted "Where the hell's that kid?" from somewhere near our bench every time one of our players almost broke his skull tripping over a bat.

A lot of kids get spanked for not picking up their toys but I'll bet Im the only guy in the world who got his whacks for not picking up bats.

I don't really know whether my dad is a frustrated ballplayer or not, but I like to think I got into playing serious baseball because he didn't bug me into playing it. He never forced me to play catch with him, or never made me practice ballplaying when I would much rather have caught worms. I started this out by inferring that parental influence doesn't have much to do with a kid's ballplaying ability, which is true. But sometimes too much influence does have an adverse effect.

When I started playing ball in any kind of organized manner, there weren't any Little Leagues yet, such as the Babe Ruth League or Colt League, which I think are a great advantage to kids nowadays. The kids get people teaching them who know what they're doing, not some father who thinks his kid is the new Sandy Koufax and who teaches little Sandy how to throw curves and knucklers when he's eleven.

Kids are too young for that stuff at that age. The father, nine times out of ten, is doing more to ruin his kid's career then help it. When you start throwing "junk"—curves, knucklers, screwballs, etc.—it invariably takes something away from your fast ball. This is probably the one fundamental lesson a guy has to learn when he's serious about following a career as a pitcher. Junk wrecks your fast ball, and the more junk you throw when you're in high school or thereabouts, the less effective your fast ball is when you really need it—when you're older.

Throwing hard is what scouts look for. A club can teach a ballplayer to run, to hit, to field, to bunt, to cover a bag; but only God gives a guy a hard throw. This goes double for a pitcher.

In fact, if you'll notice, you'll never see Sandy Koufax, Juan Marichal or Don Drysdale fooling around with knuckle balls, fork balls, or any of that stuff. It takes too much off their speed. A guy like Warren Spahn, say, keeps going—and going good—because as you get older you naturally get slower, and that's when he started doubling up on his mental game, his control. Spahnnie can slow up, throw some excellent junk, and he's got 'em baffled. And he keeps winning ball games.

But if he'd thrown all that junk sixteen years ago, he would have bowed out in Boston.

The young kids rare back and blow the ball by the batter (it says here) ; the older guys play a more scientific game. But the guys who get the chance to get old as major leaguers are the same guys who threw a good fast ball, slider, curve and change-up when they were young, not loop-the-loops, butterfly balls and figure-eights.

So Little Leagues are a good thing. I wish they'd had them when I was a kid.

I was a third baseman in junior high school. I was always a big kid (my mother would say "tall and husky") and threw the hardest because of sheer size. Our eighth grade manager needed a pitcher one day and decided on me. I stayed on the mound for a few games, and then a few more, and by the time I got to high school I was a pitcher.

I said my dad didn't bug me too much. That's not quite true. He bugged me to death about going to work in the summers; *I* was the one who wanted to play ball. We went round and round fairly often. The fact I always wound up playing ball makes me wonder a bit, now that I think about it. Is there such a thing as reverse bugging?

My dad did one thing I can remember that was an actual, positive effort to get me to play ball. He was a good friend of Eddie Malone's, a big league and PCL catcher for many years who was heading up the Seattle Rainiers when I was in high school. My dad came in one day and announced I was trying out for Eddie's team at Wrigley Field in L. A. I was excited, and nothing ever came of it, but that was the only time I can remember that my dad coerced me into playing. (Some day I'll have to ask him what he would have said had I agreed to go to work instead of playing ball those summers. He probably would have whacked me one and told me to go pick up some bats.)

My high school records were inconsistent at best. My Earned Run Average was good, and I had a lot of strikeouts, but my overall record in high school was something like 2–8. Our coach, Al Cage, who played a lot of pro ball in his heyday, told me I had a 2.18 ERA, pretty good for high school ball. We ended up way down in the cellar (later on I'd get used to it, organization-wise) in the high school leagues, and I generally had a bad win-loss record. I suppose I could give the same old pitcher's excuse and say I didn't get too much support in high school. Which is true, but I finally did go out and buy one.

I pitched some good games, though. My big problem, which was to haunt me for the rest of my career, was control. Or the lack of it. I would walk too many batters, get wild frequently, and get myself in trouble more often than anyone else did. For example, one time we played El Rancho High School and I had 18 strikeouts out of a possible 21 outs (we played seven innings in high school). The only trouble was, the score was 8–8 at the end of seven innings.

Funny thing about pitching. A guy can strike out 27 batters in nine innings, but if there's a total of 48 at-bats for the other team when the game's over, it kind of takes the edge off it all. Like getting a great shave, but losing a lip.

Recognition is important to kids. When I played high school ball, a kid who threw a no-hitter, say, might just as well have seen a flying saucer. Big deal. Nobody really cared, and nobody really saw it in the first place. A kid didn't realize then that he'd accomplished anything, aside from the pats on the back from a few teammates and that sort of thing. Nobody stood out. There were no stars.

Nowadays, a kid throws a no-hitter and it's Armageddon in the local papers. Hundreds of people read about it and the kid has something to cut out and send back east to his Uncle Willy and Aunt Helen.

I'm not knocking it. I think the interest nowadays in high school baseball is a good thing and should stay. It gives a kid something to shoot for, something to try harder for. When I was in high school we went out to play a game and there were maybe ten people watching us. Mostly mothers and girl friends, both of which thought we were playing football. I think a person—any person—does better when there are people around, people watching him and judging his work. This goes for plumbers and firemen and writers and CPA's and ballplayers. A writer writes better when people read him and criticize him; a plumber does better when the owner or contractor is inspecting his work; a ballplayer does better when the stands are full and people are ready to cheer or boo.

Naturally a guy will pitch better when there are a hundred folks in the stands then when there are only his best friend's mom, his English teacher, and Fatso Cudahy necking with his girl friend.

Just as a good crowd and a bad crowd have their particular influence on a performance—ask any entertainer! —people in the stands have an effect on a player's work during a game. That "extra effort," the "something extra," is given when you know someone cares how you're doing. Don't ever let a major league ballplayer tell you the crowd doesn't bother him. When a guy gets booed, it bothers the hell out of him even if he's hitting .350 in late September.

But in high school, the absence of a crowd doesn't *consciously* bother a guy. It's just that he plays better, inadvertently maybe, when there are people watching him.

Everyone is a ham at heart, so he'll play anyway, of course, because it's a helluva lot of fun and it beats kissing girls. At that age, I mean.

I wasn't really serious about playing pro ball until I was a senior. Even then, nobody was paying much attention to me (ERA's don't show up in box scores), so it was really just a lot of fun and something to prove passing geometry isn't everything in life.

One day Johnny Lindell, the great Yankee, who was still playing some ball then, came over to me when we were playing Mark Kepple High School in the spring of 1955. I was opposing Mike McCormick, who has since gone on to greater things. Johnny told me he was impressed with me, and that I should start thinking seriously about playing pro ball. McCormick beat me 4–0 that day, but all four runs were unearned. Still a big "L" in the box score for me, but right then I started thinking about Lindell's remarks.

The season ended and I graduated, with nobody really beating down my doors for me to sign any contracts. But maybe that was because I had the doors wide open. I played some semi-pro ball in the summer, though, and one Sunday I found myself pitching against a team comprised of Boston Red Sox rookies, guys who had signed with the Boston organization and who were naturally pretty good ballplayers. Most of them were getting ready to leave for spring training with their respective minor league clubs. I was getting ready to leave for spring planting at my dad's nursery.

Joe Stevenson, a Boston scout in that area, was watching the game. I struck out 17 men while winning a real good ball game, 2–1, and before I knew what was happening Joe was asking me if I wanted to go play ball with San Jose, in the California League. In other words, he was asking me to sign with Boston.

I was really excited, but for some insane reason, as cocky young kids will do, I acted like I wasn't interested. Don't ask me why. Later on I was to sign with the Phillies, and at the time Boston asked me to sign, the Phillies were dominating last place so consistently they might have thought it was the Promised Land. Boston, meanwhile, had been playing some pretty good ball. No, don't ask me why.

When my dad declined that offer to go up to Seattle, it was probably because, even while unborn, I had a corner on the confidence market in our family. After the game with the Boston rookies, I must have walked around like I had invented the game, because guys like Babe Herman, the Philly scout, and Rosie Gilhausen, a scout for the Pirates, were watching me wherever I played. Rosie, in fact, invited me over to Gilmore Field to try out with the Hollywood Stars.

We had something like 93 guys working out that day at Gilmore, and I ended up being one of the five guys they wanted to sign: a catcher, a third baseman, and three pitchers. I worked out with them for two more weeks, throwing batting practice, playing in inter-squad games, etc., and Bobby Bragan, the manager then, was giving me a lot of help. It was all a great thrill.

Finally Gilhausen asked my parents to come with me to

the general manager's office one night after a game. They offered me a $1,500 bonus and $250 a month to sign a contract. Me! No kidding! With the Boston Red Sox!

My folks turned the offer down. I was kind of excited about it, being the greatest pitcher since Mathewson, and I remember we had a pretty good fight about signing. I wanted to play ball, but my dad couldn't figure out how anyone could live on $250 a month. My feeling was that he'd been supporting me for 17 years, so why couldn't he supplement my $250 until I became a star? Good logic, eh?

If a son of mine ever signs for anyone for $250 a month I'll beat his brains out. But at the time, my dad was the most unreasonable man in the world and I was the maddest almost-was in semi-pro ball.

In those days—pre '56—any team who signed a guy for more than $4,000 had to play him in the majors for two years. And the team could only sign two such "bonus babies" in a year. There were a lot of under-the-table pay-offs, though. No team will let a guy go if the Powers-That-Be think he's got talent and can do the club some good in a few years. So they'd sign a kid for less than the $4,000, to keep from having to play him in the majors, but they compensated the guy unofficially just to get him, period.

I know one guy who took the White Sox for $20,000, just stringing them along, and then up and signed with the Phillies. The White Sox had to eat the loss, because they couldn't blow the whistle on the kid without exposing themselves.

Nowadays they sign a player for $100,000 without

batting an eye, just because he can run and hit. I guess if a guy just looks good, or has a well-oiled glove, he'll get at least ten grand to sign. The game has changed a lot since '55.

Frank Howard got about $103,000 to sign with the Dodgers a few years back, and a kid named Bob Garibaldi was signed by the Giants for $150,000. Howard's playing, but he's no great shakes. Garibaldi has only pitched a few innings of major league baseball in a little over two years. Seems a lot of money to pay for potential. If I sound bitter, you're right. If it was *my* potential, that dough would be an adequate bonus.

I can't ever remember seeing the Final Standings with a "Should Have Won" column, that's why I'm a little peeved. I like money, sure, but I got offered $1,500 and $250 a month. I just can't get used to the idea that that makes me worth three-twentieths of Frank Howard and one-hundredth of Bob Garibaldi.

There is a great paradox here, which I never hear spoken about or proclaimed in our sports journals. It's this: The bonus system gives a kid a good break, because when a team is willing to invest a lot of dough in him, the team will usually give the kid a chance to make it in the majors—they won't give up on him so soon. But on the other hand, if a kid gets $100,000 or $150,000 it tends to destroy his initiative—why the hell beat your brains out playing ball when you've just been handed more money than the average American makes in ten years?

Yeah, I know. I should have held out.

Babe Herman, who is probably the greatest guy I met

ın six years of pro ball, started watching me more closely after that Red Sox deal. I didn't find out until a few years ago that, way back in '55 Babe traveled all the way to San Bernardino just to take a look at me. Later on, the great Dodger slugger and all-around helluva nice guy was to play an important part in trying to make a major leaguer out of Jerry Kettle.

Babe came out to the house one night and sat down with my folks. I never got included in this one, even though I was a seventeen-year-old financial wizard. Like Bob Garibaldi, right?

When the caucus was over, the Philadelphia Phillies, Lords of the Cellar since the '50 Whiz Kids, were offering me $4,000 and $350 a month to sign with them. All of a sudden my dad was brilliant.

A lot of people ask me what it feels like to be offered all that money (*sic*) to play professional baseball, sort of the All-American Dream type of thing. I'm sorry, but I don't remember. This was right before I turned eighteen, and all I wanted to do was play baseball. I guess I would have signed for free, but my folks and Babe worked out an equitable agreement. I was too excited to jot down my feelings, and Babe, being the fairest guy you could ever hope to do business with, was almost as excited as I.

Looking back on it now, I guess I still get excited, but I was just a dinky kid at the time. The greatest pitcher in baseball, but still just a dinky kid.

Nobody will ever offer me as much money in a lump again, unless I sell him a house or something. The very act of signing on the dotted line is something of a maturation process, but you never can quite put your finger on it until many years later. You can always see mistakes better after they're made, whether it's throwing a fast ball when you should have changed up, or not signing with the right club.

There are two schools of thought on this one. One contends that it's better to sign with a lousy club, like the Phillies were through most of the Fifties, because you get a better chance to make the Biggies. Signing, say, with the New York Yankees, who constantly dominate that other league over there—I forget the name of it—would seem to eliminate most of the chances at getting a crack at it, because the team itself is comprised of the best around. The competition is tougher, and as long as a team is winning pennants, why should they bring up a young kid who's never pitched a major league inning? On the other hand, a lousy team will try each player's grandmother to get the hell out of a cellar.

The other school contends that *because* the competition is tougher and the parent club is better, a kid learns faster and becomes better ultimately than when he's pitching with some dink cellar-club organization. If I was forced to pin myself down, though, I'd advise a kid to sign with the lousier club. Casey Stengel said last year that his team, the New York Mets, gives a kid a better opportunity to make the Biggies because Casey so desperately needs talent. I sort of agree with him. But it *is* tougher, don't forget, to *stay* up there with a lousy club than it is with a good one. If the pennant winner brings you up in the first place, you're good, brother, damn good. Going up with the Mets, however, might be a little like playing handball in a roomful of bear traps.

Fifty grand or so helps a kid make up his mind, though. Or his parents' minds.

Anyway, I can pinpoint one mistake I made during that period, but it falls into the second-guessing class. I had enrolled in Citrus Junior College in the fall of '55, but wasn't very much interested in school. I played basketball for the school, and played semi-pro ball on Sundays on a team managed by my basketball coach, Bob Waters. It was a top-notch club and I worked some pretty good games. But when I signed with the Phils, I dropped out of school and off Waters' team, to get ready to leave in February for Philadelphia's rookie school.

Waters' team went on to win a 21-team invitational tournament that spring, a pretty good thing for a local team and something which attracts scouts like flies. I think if I'd stayed on that team for another few months, I might have got a better offer than the one with the Phils. As I said, second guessing, but the year I went with the Phils was the year they changed the bonus rule, and my finishing on Waters' winning team just might have brought in a much higher bonus.

In January, shortly before we were to leave for Clearwater, Florida, Babe Herman took a few of us from Southern California and worked us out in a local park to get us in shape. We ran, threw batting practice, ran some more, played lots of pepper, practiced bunting and then ran some more. I'd like to say a few choice words about Babe Herman at this point, because he worked us as if we were his own sons trying to make a team.

Babe was a great hitter for the Brooklyn Dodgers, one of the best the team ever had. He is also probably the nicest guy that or any other team ever had. The only flaw in the Babe Herman entity is the fact that he couldn't field worth a damn, as great a hitter as he was. One time— I guess everyone's heard the story—Babe chased a fly ball and it wound up hitting him right smack on the head. Which is better than getting hit in a lot of other places. Like in the ninth inning.

The difference between Babe and any other scout, as far as I'm concerned, is that Babe *sounds* like he wants you to play ball with his organization. He *looks* like he wants you to play. Back when I was talking to the Pirates and Red Sox, the guys sounded sincere, sure; they sounded like they wanted me to play with them. But with Babe, I don't know, he just sounded like your playing ball with his club was to him something like having Sonny Liston on your side in a fight. Not that he snowed you, or over-exaggerated the potential, but he simply said he liked you and that his club would be glad to have you and, by God, it *sounded* like it.

Later in my career, especially when things were going bad and I was ready to quit, my dad's letters would cheer me up and offer some encouragement. And every single letter I got would mention how Babe called that week and asked how I was doing, suggesting to my dad things he could say to cheer me up and get me to hang in there.

A couple of times Babe even came to the house, had dinner, and talked to my dad about me.

Whatever gripe I have about the Phillies or about my own attitudes, you'll never hear a word from my mouth about Babe Herman that doesn't sound like I'm talking about the Holy Ghost.

Let's put it this way. Babe was a far better man than he was a hitter. Whenever I think about that fly ball story, I feel a little sad because I know Babe was trying like hell and . . .

Oh, what the hell. If I'm sounding schmaltzy, you're right. That's how I feel about Babe. I'd swear on a stack of Bibles that the percentage Babe would get from signing any ballplayer was probably the farthest thing from his mind. I've heard of some scouts who sound like cash registers when they cough and have irises the color of dollars. But I'm certain Babe, when he passes from here and leaves a large empty space in baseball's world, will be standing there at the Judgment and start out by saying, "Well, I'll tell you, Lord. My first mistake was in choking up a mite too high . . ."

Anyway, before the five of us boarded the plane for the Phillies' rookie school, Babe had us in pretty decent shape and we'd already learned a few minor points about How to Be a Big League Ballplayer for Fun and Profit. Mostly fun.

There were five of us leaving. Chuck Essegian was one (he finally made it to the Biggies), and a catcher from the University of Southern California named Dick Harris, who was to become one of my best friends. I can't remember the others.

Of course, there was a lot of excitement around my house. Relatives and friends would drop over and gape at me, usually cooing something like "Well, how's Bob Feller today?" or "Can you get us free passes when the Phils get in town?"

Cocky Kettle lapped it up, naturally, and the following piece by Kent Hekenraft in the Monrovia *News-Post* certainly didn't help my modesty any:

KETTLE SIGNS BASEBALL CONTRACT WITH PHILS

Ex-MD Pitcher to Play with Class B Club

Former Monrovia High School athlete, Jerry Kettle, has signed a contract to pitch for the Philadelphia Phillies Baseball Club.

The 6-foot, 4-inch fireball specialist celebrated his 18th birthday this week with the much anticipated news that he will be heading for the Phillies' big youth training camp at Clearwater, Fla., Feb. 7.

Philadelphia scout, Babe Herman, quite a ballplayer in his own heyday, chose Kettle as one of three prospects to send to Florida, along with a substantial bonus. The lanky Duartean is one of the elite 39 selected from the entire nation to attend the three-week tryouts in Clearwater.

Play in Class B

After three weeks of training, Jerry will bid "See ya later, alligator" to Florida and start playing organized ball in a Class B league, where he will receive valuable baseball nuggets of information from many of the former baseball greats and coaches that are affiliated with the Phillies' vast youth campaign organization.

It will be interesting to follow the local boy's career as he has great potential. When "Jake" worked out with the Hollywood Stars last summer, pilot Bobby Bragan remarked that Kettle was one of the best major league prospects he'd ever seen.

MONROVIA—DUARTE STANDOUT

So Jerry should be joining Robin Roberts & Co. before too long and commence to carve a notch for himself in the baseball world.

"Jake" graduated from Monrovia High last year where he was a standout on the baseball and basketball squads. He now attends Citrus Junior College and will finish the semester there before setting his sights for Florida.

Jerry lives with his parents, Mr. and Mrs. S. W. Kettle, who reside at 1636 Brightside Ave., Duarte. Mr. Kettle owns a nursery in Pasadena.

Yessir, boy. Don't knock hometown newspapers.

It sure was interesting following the local boy's career. Thanks, anyway, Bobby. Thanks, Kent. And thanks, Phillies. With a few more brains in your organization, you might have had yourself a pretty good local boy of a pitcher. Or should I say organization in your brains?

2

Eddie Miller's Miracle

My first pro ball thrill was the plane ride to Florida—I'd never been on a plane before. We all went down to L. A. International Airport and boarded an American Airlines jet. The trip was to take us to Dallas (Texas), New Orleans and Tampa, but I didn't get much of a view of those places. However, I can give an incredibly accurate description of the inside of a whoopee cup.

We went by limousine from Tampa to Clearwater, where the rookie school is set up and where the Phillies take their spring training each year. The rookie school is actually just an organized shaper-upper for the most promising new talent, not necessarily rookies. I reported to rookie school again in '57, '58 and '59, and it was invariably a fine way to get in shape and work out the winter kinks.

Rookie school that first year was pretty rugged. In high school, we'd go out after school and play ball until it got dark. In Clearwater, they had some nut leading calisthenics, some other screwball making everyone in sight run his brains out, and an assortment of other guys throwing gloves, balls, bats and advice at you whenever you stopped to catch your breath. Some of us called the place Stalag 8. The 8 stood for the Phils' position in the Final Standings each year.

We went out about ten in the morning and worked until about three, with a half hour for lunch. And when you're playing ball six hours a day, every day, it gets to be a little different from what Great Fun baseball is generally thought to be. It's a helluva grind and it gets to be just like any other job, if you'll pardon my cliché. Punching a clock in a white collar job is no different, and it's a lot less tiring. Besides, you sweat less, too.

All the minor league managers show up at rookie school, plus a few of the Biggie club's coaches, so they always have something for you to do. Like run. Whenever they're all stumped for some new thing to make you do, they tell you to run. When you've stopped running, they usually have it figured out. Run some more.

Aside from running, you're constantly being told to grab a bat, or play some pepper, or "Get the hell up to the bunting machine, twenty-three!" One hour you'll be shagging flies in the outfield, to make you sweat and keep your legs tuned up; another hour you'll be on the sidelines playing catch to loosen up your arm. Maybe you'll throw batting practice a few days, or maybe you'll spend a whole day fielding ground balls and bunts. Then there's running from foul line to foul line across the out-field, to make you sweat. There's also practicing your throw to first, or covering that bag on a grounder to first. Oh, there are lots of things a pitcher does. Sometimes he even pitches.

After we got into pretty decent shape, we did a lot of what is called "situation playing." In this, a guy will set up an actual game condition, such as having runners on first and third, one out, you on the mound, and he'll lash a single through the right side. You're supposed to do whatever it is you're supposed to be doing. On the field, I mean. In that particular case, a pitcher would run over and back up third. The guy on third is going to score, but you don't want that rear runner getting anything he's not entitled to, like scoring if the throw goes past the third baseman.

The situation plays were kind of fun and it was good to be playing real ball again, even if it wasn't competitive. I learned a lot and got into fabulous shape. I came down to Clearwater at 190 lbs., and two weeks later I was down 170, a pretty good drop. I'd be classified as a big pitcher, along the Don Drysdale lines. Right now I'm 6'5" and 220 lbs. In my best playing days I wasn't much lighter and had already reached my height. But at Clearwater, I felt like Superman.

The only trouble was, the Phillies thought I looked more like John Carradine. They had a good friend of mine, Dick Harris, take me out each afternoon and buy me a few beers to keep my weight up. I may not have made any indelible marks in the record books, but there's a beer hall owner in Clearwater that won't bet against me in a chug-a-lug contest.

Living conditions at rookie school were great and nothing like the crummy conditions I was to see in most other minor league ball. The Phillies stayed at the Fort Harrison Hotel, and we rookies stayed in smaller hotels around. This wasn't such great shakes, but we had our dinners and breakfast at the Harrison. We weren't getting any money, but room and board were all we needed. We were too tired in the evenings to think of hitting the town or some other entertainment. (That's okay, I don't believe it either.)

Playing conditions were good and also nothing like we'd see later on in the minors. The field was in good shape, the grass was trimmed, boulders were absent from the outfield, the mound was approximately in the center of the infield, and first base was 90 ft. away from the plate.

All the routine things, the pepper games, the calisthenics, etc., got pretty boring, but occasionally a good day on the mound would brighten up the atmosphere. Naturally I got to know the pitchers first, and we all used to moan and groan about not doing any pitching. If a guy had a good day, though—which you can just *feel*, regardless of whether you actually played competitively— he couldn't wait to get back out the next day. Bad days were equally, if oppositely, stimulating. When a guy rode you or pointed out a particularly stupid thing you did, like spike a coach while crossing a bag, it put you down in the dumps for a while. Young kids, most away from home for the first time, and we were pretty sensitive. We looked for compliments like vultures.

The Big Leaguers, or most of them, didn't come to camp until about March 1. Some would come earlier, to get into shape sooner, but we didn't see too many. Each year some guys in rookie school were invited to stay over and work out with the Phillies in spring training. This was an especially big deal, and we all hoped we'd be among the five or so asked to stay over. I was invited over in '57 and '58 but, as you'll see, '56 wasn't my year. In fact, it was the same kind of year for me as it was for Adlai Stevenson.

It's exciting to get invited over to spring training with the Phils. We even got into the financial squabbles. One time, in '57, it was noticed that the Phillies were getting $67 a week for entertainment, etc., but the kids invited to stay over weren't getting a cent. Some of the minor league managers raised a big stink about it. You know, equal rights type of thing. I remember Paul Owens and Frank Lucchesi, two great guys, spoke to the organization and came in one day to tell us we were getting the same $67 as the big leaguers, starting immediately. It was like getting blood from a turnip, though. It seems that, while it was a great thrill and honor to be invited to stay, the Phillies expected us to live on thrill and honor while we were there. But Lucchesi and Owens got us the dough, so it didn't develop into one of the many inequities and injustices that the minor leaguer has to put up with.

I played with some pretty good names in those days. Don Cardwell, Dennis Bennett, Chuck Essegian, Art Mahaffey, Dallas Green, Bobby Wine, to name a few. We had some good times, too, especially when we found ourselves on various A- and B-team rosters. The Cardinals, who trained at St. Petersburg, would send over a team to Clearwater, and we'd send one to St. Pete. There were always two squads going, so you got a good chance to play some competitive ball rather than just work out on the field.

But that was in '57. In '56 I never even saw a big leaguer and, as I said, didn't get invited to stay over with the Phillies.

After rookie school that first year I was sent over to Plant City to play with the Miami club, a Triple-A team. I was signed to play with a Class B team, though, which meant I probably wouldn't stay in Triple-A ball for long. But rather than send me home, the Phils shuffled me over to the Triple-A camp because it was opening up a week after the Phil camp opened. Minor league clubs train later and open the season later than in the majors. The lower down the totem pole you go, the later the camp opens. The Phils liked me at the time, and wanted me to keep throwing. So there I was in Triple-A ball with a B contract. Quite sobering. Literally.

I was right. Green, but right. When the A and B camp opened, I was sent there. The A team was Schenectady, in the Eastern League, and the B team was Wilson, N. C., in the Carolina League. Dick Carter managed the A team and Charlie Gassoway skippered Wilson. Frank Lucchesi was also there, because he managed Salt Lake City, a Class

C team, and was looking things over before his team
started up the season.

We trained there for a while, playing inter-squad
games, and I was finally optioned to Salt Lake City, the
C team. Lucchesi grabbed me up, and this is where I first
got to know him. Since I was to play about four seasons
with Frank, all the way up to A ball, I may as well say a
few things about this fabulous and whacky baseball man.

Frank Lucchesi, in the off season, is a bartender in San
Francisco. He does what ballplayers do *during* the season.
Makes drinks.

Frank had a small medical problem. He was hit several
times while playing ball, and now has a steel plate in his
head. Once in a while, when it was real hot in the towns
we played in, Frank would faint and get a bit sick.

But Frank is a real fine manager and a smart baseball
man. He's also quite a showman. One time, after we'd had
a fight on the field with the Cards' team, Winston-Salem,
Frank was thrown out of the game. As he walked past the
plate umpire, he pickpocketed the ump's whisk broom.
Now, just as a ballplayer needs a glove, a banker needs
money and Candy Barr needs her lungs, an umpire needs
a whisk broom.

So Frank got it from him—I forget who the ump was—
and when he left the dugout he stayed just inside the
doorway to peek out at the field. Before leaving, however,
he had kicked dirt all over home plate, which is a pretty
standard thing to do. Like no laughs at all.

But the ump, as all umps will do (talk about *showmen!*)
when they decide to whisk off home plate, walked out in

front of the plate, turned around, and was in the process of stooping over when he reached for his whisk broom. He was almost all the way down when he discovered he was only scratching his ass in front of 2,000 fans. You think the crowd roared when Ben-Hur won that race? You should have heard this one when the ump tried to act casual and strolled around the infield grass looking for his whisk broom!

Finally Lucchesi did the only thing you can do to follow an act like that. He walked out and handed the ump his broom. The place went wild. The visiting team's manager was the hero of the day. They loved him.

Whenever Frank, who coached third base, waved in a winning run and knew the guy would be safe, he'd stand on his head in the coach's box. The fans would go wild over this. It got so nobody—even the opposing team— would look at the home umpire for the call. They'd look at Frank and if he was standing on his head, the winning run had scored. What a way to call a play. (What a way to play a call?)

I'll make anyone a bet. Frank Lucchesi will be a major league manager some day. A buck a shot, all takers. Just write to the publisher and he'll forward your bet. The only reason Frank isn't a major league manager already is because he's so young—he's only in his mid-thirties. When I played for him, he was the youngest manager around, and he had a record of never finishing below third place in ten years. I wish I could say that.

Yeah, I know, Gene Mauch. Gene's a good guy and a good manager, don't get me wrong. It's just that Gene played major league ball, and Frank never did. So who the hell's going to listen to a young guy who never played in the Biggies telling him how to play? Frank's going to be a major league manager because he's brilliant and because he can handle men. But, unfortunately, Frank will have to be old before he'll make it. What the hell, did you ever see a teen-age senior citizen?

I remember when Frank used to tell me to suit up early for a game, and for the first few times I couldn't figure out why. But then he'd go out on the field with me and I'd throw at him and he'd bat, about 30 feet away from me. Sometimes he'd tap the ball so I had to move in fast, sometimes he'd try to wham it by me, or skull me with a line drive. Good fielding training, which I needed, when all Frank had to do was sit there and act like a manager. Sometimes it was real hot and Frank knew he was taking a chance at overtaxing that plate in his head, but he'd be out there anyway cracking a ball at poor-fielding Jerry Kettle. Good for your reflexes, but bad for your underwear.

Well, more about Frank later. I first met him with the Salt Lake City C team, and we were to become good friends for many years later.

In these days, by the way, all I had was a fast ball and a curve. They were teaching me the change-up, but those two pitches were actually all I was throwing. I was still having control problems, even with just two pitches, but Whitlow Wyatt, a great coach and another great guy, aided me immensely with my control and my whole movement.

(Whit's now in Milwaukee, I believe; the Philly organization lost a good man when they let him go.)

At that age, you never become reluctant to listen to advice. The individual attention in spring training is probably the best thing going for the young rookie. To have a major league great like, say, Whitlow Wyatt show me what I was doing wrong was a tremendous thrill. I'd cling to every word he said, and I even remember watching him throw while demonstrating a point, and wondering whether I'd ever be as great as he was. I guess I wondered about a lot of things in those days. Like how I'd get home if I got canned, for instance.

I got bombed in five innings in the first game at Salt Lake City. I had poor stuff, no control and was generally going downhill from the first batter. My first start in pro ball, and I was a nervous wreck. A green, nervous wreck. They accepted the fact that I was nervous, thank God, so nothing really mattered about my record in that game. I did get discouraged, though. Four or five thousand people in the stands and I get bombed. What a debut!

I was consoled slightly by my friend Dick Harris, who was having his own problems. One day we had a guy named Mark Sampson pitching for us, a fellow who was aptly named. Mark threw just about the hardest on the team, but was wild as hell. (*There* was a consolation, too. I was only the *second* wildest.) Mark had been put in in the late innings, because we were beating the hell out of the Cardinals' team and they wanted him to get some work. They also put in Harris, to check him out, too. When Mark came in he threw 13 consecutive balls,

loading the bases and getting one behind the fourth batter. Half of his pitches had hit the backstop. The fourth
batter, after seeing one go by and crack into the backstop
screen, probably wondered about his life insurance, because he suddenly stepped out of the box right before
Mark's next pitch. The ump called time, and Harris just
squatted there on his haunches looking over at the dugout.

Only trouble was, Mark hadn't heard time called, and
threw the ball. Harris turned around when he heard
everyone shouting, but it was too late. Mark had thrown
his first goddam strike and Harris caught it with his mask.
He went down on his ass, out like a light.

Five minutes later Harris woke up, groaning and cursing out Sampson. We could all see Harris wasn't hurt,
so someone leaned down and whispered to him, "Strike
one." Dick responded with an equally metered phrase,
but it had nothing to do with baseball. Well, almost nothing.

That night Dick and I were out boozing, and Dick
bought his mask a beer. He'd brought it with him, promising he was going to sleep with it, and he set it on the
bar top telling the bartender to give it a beer. When it
finally came—after some interesting looks from a few local
patrons—Dick would say, "Drink up, ol' buddy" and
pour beer on the mask. Then he'd put his arm around it
and tell it a few jokes, laughing at each one. Now, I know
catcher's masks are useful things, but maybe whoever
whispered "strike one" had something there.

It was about ten days later when Frank put me in to

relieve against Idaho Falls, the Tigers' club, and I had real good stuff. I threw some fabulous pitches and my control was excellent. I also got bombed again, worse than the last time. Some days you can't win, as we say in the trade.

Naturally, after this sterling performance, when the 30-day cutdown came Kettle was high on the list. They wanted to send me to the California League, which was also C ball, but they finally decided to send me to D ball so I'd get the chance to pitch every four days or so. Lucchesi bid me farewell and bet me $5 I'd be back up on the higher teams before long. (I don't think I ever paid him.)

D ball is an experience everyone should try. The ball parks are firetraps and look like they'll collapse right after the next fast ball. I was sent to Mattoon, Illinois, a town that's hard to believe. If I were going to give the United States an enema, I'd put the tube in Mattoon.

We had to dress for the game in two platoons, the quarters were so small. The uniforms were hand-me-downs from the Phillies, suits that were about five or six years old but were patchable. I think Goodwill must have turned them down, so the Phillies sent them over to the D ballplayers.

We even traveled in three station wagons. When I think of the Biggies sending their players around in jets and putting them up in the best hotels, I always think back to D ball. Picture 19 ballplayers and a manager, not to mention our equipment, traveling around in three station wagons. That may have been some incentive to bear down and make it to the Biggies, but I think it was more depressing than anything else. A guy can't play ball very well when he's got cramps from traveling, his suit's two sizes too small and the gophers are running all over the infield. *With* the ball. I'd bet a lot of potentially good ballplayers quit the game and went home because of the conditions in D, C and B ball. Incentive, they say. The only people getting incentive at Mattoon were station wagon dealers.

So there I was in Mattoon, in the Mid-West League. Vinnie Zintera was the manager, an old Cincinnati infielder.

To start off, I pulled the old act again in my first game at Mattoon. I got bombed all over the place. Thank God I was still young. And green. It was a big letdown going from rookie school in Clearwater to Mattoon in D ball but it all rolled off—sort of—and I was just happy to still be playing ball.

By this time I'd had a lot behind me, actually. I'd gone from rookie school to a Triple-A camp, to an A and B camp, to a C club, and down to a D club. I was a wizened veteran, it says here. I started at the top and worked my way down. I was even tying my shoelaces backwards.

The letdown was only in the conditions, though. The playing was all the same to me. My eighteen-year-old mind was more impressed with having to change in a car rather than a locker room, or having my jock and glove the only equipment still in one piece.

Anyway, my colossal career was looking pitifully short. I lost my first six or seven games at Mattoon. Mattoon, yet! God, I was glad that writer from the Monrovia *News-Post* wasn't *really* following the local boy's career!

I wasn't even throwing good games. None of this 2–1 or 1–0 stuff for Kettle, no sir. I'd be out in two or three innings and about five runs behind.

Dammit, there was nobody there to help me. By this time I was realizing I wasn't any Bob Feller or Sandy Koufax, and that I wouldn't be up in the Biggies immediately, winning games and signing autographs. I needed help. No kid learns to pitch by himself, regardless of what they all say or how many How To Pitch books you read. A young kid on the ropes needs help, and I was getting none of it. I knew I needed it, too. The more I pitched, the more trouble I'd get into, and finally Zintera would come out with the hook.

No blame is to be placed on Vinnie. What the hell is an infielder—and a good one, too—supposed to know about what's wrong with a pitcher? How the hell can a manager who's got 18 other guys to worry about devote much time to an ailing pitcher? If the major league organizations had more coaches in the lesser minors, they'd produce some better talent. If a kid gets the instruction *when he needs it,* his chances of making a better go of it as he gets higher up are much better. Spend some money for God's sake, and send a few good coaches down to D and C ball. So your new bonus baby gets about five grand less.

One night in Mattoon, when I was about 0–4 so far, and when I eased up to get the ball over the plate, they'd got my first real coaching—from a chair. I was real wild, belt it out of the park. When I got the hook and went into the clubhouse, I was determined to quit. I remember composing a please-send-plane-fare wire to my dad in my mind. I was so mad I picked up a folding chair to throw it through half-a-mirror we had on one wall, but the thing swung out and knocked me in the mouth so hard I lost half a tooth and reeled back against a wall. That sobered me for a while, but it didn't strike me until much later that that chair was the only bit of coaching I'd had since arriving in that hick berg.

Let me tell you about frustration. I wanted to win a ball game so bad I could taste it, but there wasn't a goddam soul within a thousand miles who could tell me what I was doing wrong. Throughout the rest of my career in baseball, I was never so frustrated or more willing to give up the game and take up ballet.

In fact, the first game I won with Mattoon was one time in Michigan City when we pulled one out 9–3, but I'd walked 13 men. How's *that* for a smashing effort? I'd struck out 14, but that'll show you what kind of games I was throwing.

So I was 2–8 at Mattoon, with three weeks left in the season, and in the biggest rut ever worn. They called me in one day and told me they were sending me down to Tifton, Georgia, to finish out the season. Tifton was another D team, with Eddie Miller managing. Eddie was a real good second baseman in his time, and a sort of troubleshooter for the Phillies. Eddie had been sent to Tifton to finish up the season when the previous manager, Wes Griffin, passed away.

Eddie was a fabulous baseball man, and had some good theories on baseball. He was always in hot water with the organization, which for some reason seemed to think no one really understood the game unless he was following Philly policy. Eddie's only "mistake" was that he'd open his mouth and give an opinion, which invariably ran contradictory to what was going on at the time. For instance, a manager or other bigwig would tell a pitcher to go work on his fast ball and Eddie would come up with something like "The hell with his fast ball. He's already got a good one. Let him work on his curve."

"The fast ball's his best pitch. Tell him to work on it," the expert would say.

Eddie would just shrug his shoulders and shout, "Go work on that curve, kid."

Eddie was either fired or induced to quit later, in '57. The Phils lost a good man, then, but what the hell? They let Whitlow Wyatt go, didn't they?

When I got to Tifton, it took Eddie Miller about six microseconds to notice what I was doing wrong. I was raising my head while pulling my left (glove) arm back during my delivery. In others words, I was tilting back and having to peek over my shoulder at the plate, instead of just coiling my whole body by pivoting on my right foot. The coiling motion gives you a lot of extra zoom, as well as making your motion a lot smoother.

There weren't even two weeks left, but I won three games for Tifton in nine days. I could do no wrong. I lost my first start, which was when Eddie noticed my flaw, but the next three were breezes. I beat the first-place team

5–4 in nine innings; I beat the Brunswick Pirates, the Pittsburgh club, 1–0 on five hits, and I beat the Dodger club down there 10–5, again going all the way. I felt like I could have pitched every third game until Christmas, and maybe lost just one. When I had a cold or something.

So I finished '56 in good fashion, even though my record, which was all in D ball, was 5–9. I was going great guns when it was all over, which is a helluva help when you report next season. God bless Eddie Miller. Eddie Miller and Babe Herman.

God bless Mommy and Daddy and my little brother and Eddie Miller and Babe Herman.

3

⊖

Reflections of a Rookie

*P*laying professional baseball can be like sitting in a bathtub; after you get used to it, it's not so hot.

All through that first season I was writing fairly regularly to my dad, and in almost every letter he sent me there would be some mention of how Babe Herman phoned or stopped at the house to check on how I was coming along. Babe would get my dad to encourage me as much as possible, and try to get me to understand that the first year is always the toughest, don't even *think* of quitting—that sort of thing. Many times a Herman-inspired line in a letter would make a big difference in whether I'd have another go with that folding chair. Brosnan was right. Some seasons seem like they'll *never* end.

In general, except for the sheer horror of my performance, nothing impressed me too greatly that first year. I was impressed by the novelty of it all, mostly—something like being in a courtroom for the first time. I'd worked out or played with a variety of clubs, got an excellent pitching tip from Eddie Miller, and generally managed to stumble wide-eyed through the season.

I was a pro ballplayer, though, which in itself is a pretty damn good feeling. Too bad the feeling wore off after rookie school.

The Philly organization seemed good enough, although I hadn't any experiences to compare it with. Boston paid their troops a lot more dough, I'd heard, but I didn't really care one way or the other. At that time, that is.

I noticed a funny thing that first year in the minors. The old question of whether it's good or bad playing for an organization that has a monopoly on last place, as the Phils did, came up often among the players themselves. I think when a team's parent club is finishing in last place more regularly than George Lincoln Rockwell, it affects the players all the way down the line. While we'd play as hard, really, there didn't seem to be that little extra bizzazz on the field, that hustle or spirit or whatever you want to call it. Not exactly sloughing off, but a lot of guys didn't really look forward to playing as much as I did, on most occasions.

Not that, on most occasions, I looked forward to playing, mind you—with a record like mine that year I didn't even look forward to sleeping. But it just didn't seem like most of the guys—on all the teams I played with—were fired up as much as they might have been.

When the parent club is finishing strong there's a buzz, an electric excitement, running all through the farm system. We could even feel it from across the field when we played the leading teams' farm clubs. Guys are hustling, trying to get up there and share some of that pennant moola. Last-place club farm teams don't seem to have it. It's kind of like being in the Army, where everything that happens is just another reason to grumble and gripe and you do something in a mediocre fashion as a matter of policy.

Another thing that may affect a guy's development and performance is that in the minors, teams are not really equal. I don't mean like the first-place and last-place clubs in the majors aren't equal; I mean like in the minors you might have a team comprised of bums playing a team comprised of sharpies—*by design*. Often, if a town is a good attendance town, say, it may have a team made up of damn good ballplayers because the parent organization wants to win a pennant there and make some dough off the gate. Your team, on the other hand, may be full of has-beens and eighteen-year-olds who are just playing ball and don't really care about winning a pennant. And in the minors, if you don't have a contending team the people don't come out to see you. Except when they have free passes.

In '61 at Chattanooga I noticed it on a large scale. Chattanooga is a funny baseball town. It's one of those places where a committee runs the club; a board of directors, like. It's a community-owned franchise, run by a sort of Booster Club. Our team had been given a hard time by these committeemen, guys who didn't know baseball from *What's My Line?* Philadelphia finally told them to keep the hell out of it, to leave the club alone, and if they did so Philly would guarantee them a pennant every year. The Boosters agreed, and Philly sent down some fine ballplayers, and we won the championship and made lots of money on attendance and the Boosters had their dinners and drooled over the players. Nice arrangement. Nice financially, I mean, but sometimes it leaves a lot to be desired in developing a young kid's talent.

For example, how would *you* like to be playing Double-A ball only because the Mayor of Chattanooga wants to get reelected?

Another impression I got that first year, which will stay with me a long, long time, is when I played in front of a large crowd for the first time in my life. Opening night in Salt Lake City was probably the high point of the season. That is, until the ump yelled "Play ball!"

There were about 5,000 in the stands—people I'd never seen before and who didn't know me from Casey Stengel. We were playing Great Falls, the Dodger club, and each player was announced by name on the public address system before the game. We'd trot out and stand along the base lines as our names were called, and if you don't think *that* does something for a kid . . . man! Crowd cheering and everything.

It had its drawback, though. I couldn't help thinking, "What the hell's this roar for? I haven't even *done* anything yet!" Ah, youth. I was thinking that exact same thought the first time I pitched there.

You remember, that night I got bombed? My first time out in Salt Lake City? Yeah, that's the one. We were playing Missoula, an independent ball club. I was a nervous wreck—we had about 2,000 in the stands that night, a new manager watching me, and I was still on my way down through my Triple-A to D reverse dash to stardom. I was wild as hell. I hit two batters, knocked down three, and banged a few dents in the backstop. The only thing I didn't hit was the center field wall, and then only because it was too far away.

Then there's the booing. These little dinky towns (let's hear a cheer from the Salt Lake City fans!) are just like miniature major league towns in this respect. They ride a guy as if he were throwing a World Series. A young guy who boots a few balls or walks three men in a row feels pretty bad about it, but these fans make him out like the Hunchback of Notre Dame. And the kid already feels worse than a major leaguer would, because he still hasn't made it yet and thinks the world's coming to an end. Nobody likes to think he'll spend the rest of his life in Mattoon, say. That booing can sure sound final.

The booing is good for development, though, paradoxically. A kid can have two attitudes. He can get angry, resenting the 2,000 experts in the stands, and become smart-alecky about his professional status (screw you, buddy; who offered *you* a contract?). Or he can bear down a little more and get back in their good graces by not kicking the ball again (I'll show these bastards what I *really* can do!).

Of course, when you adopt the latter attitude and try

like hell and then boot *another* one—man, they really get on you! You may as well have hemlock with your hamburgers after the game. But in five or six years you get hardened. When they give you your release, they're giving it to a hardened veteran.

Tricks of the trade. Every trade has its tricks, they say, and baseball's no exception. Playing that first year in '56, I naturally caught on to a few subtleties of the game. Like beaning batters.

Many times—and I admit to this myself—a pitcher will get mad enough at a batter to try to actually hit him. Not to hurt him seriously, or put one down his throat, but just to hit him a little. There are times, just out of sheer meanness—maybe you gave up a grand slammer, or you don't think the ump has been bearing down, or the opposing bench is riding you to death—that you hit a batter. On purpose. Hit him in the side, say, or in the ass. Not to kill him; just to teach him some respect. So what if the poor guy's innocent? You've just gotta hit him, that's all.

I have never heard a manager or coach tell a pitcher to bean a guy, or even to hit him. I *have* heard, however, a manager come out to the mound and say, "Jeez, this guy's been hitting us pretty good today, Jerry. Why don't you throw a tight one and loosen him up a bit." Herein lies the seed of a beautiful strategic move.

"Loosening a hitter up" is another way of saying "if he doesn't get the hell out of the way he'll get killed." It's designed to scare a batter to death. The theory goes that if a guy has had three triples off you or some other such disregard for your authority, he's real cocky and digs in solid to go after his fourth. Loosening him up—throwing a hummer at the tip of his nose—makes him think twice about digging in again. Getting out of the way of a fast ball under the chin or in on the fists—a jammer—takes a lot of speed and reflex, true, but it also takes loose feet.

The trouble with this theory is that the really good hitters, the .300 naturals, won't scare in the first place and nine times out of ten will still blast you if you're not careful. The only guys you'll scare with a knockdown pitch are the weak guys and greenies who probably haven't been hitting you at all to begin with. Ever see Willy Mays get scared and "loosen up"? Damn right, you haven't. Yet he's the guy who probably has been "loosened up" more often than anyone since Maxie Rosenbloom.

My theory is, if you want to scare a guy, hit him. Odds are you'll consider yourself lucky to let him off with only one base.

When a pitcher is really trying to hurt somebody, and there are some of this type, he'll throw just behind the batter's head, not at him. The natural reflex is to duck back, which is right into the path of an honest-to-goodness beanball. And according to Kettle's First Law, anything *other* than an honest-to-goodness beanball is a wasted pitch. May as well ask the ump to mark up another ball and save your arm.

But they don't emphasize that too much the first few years. That's something you pick up by association, like gonorrhea. They don't want to start young pitchers out

on the wrong foot (heh, heh; a pun!). He'll get his head
the first years, and later on he learns the refinements.

Spitballs are fun, too. Here again, I've never known
anyone to *teach* a kid to load one up once in a while, but
it's done on a large scale. I played with one guy, who's
now in the majors, who loaded up about every third pitch
and probably still does.

Some can get away with it easier than others. A guy
like Lew Burdette, who's fidgety and always moving
around—touching his cap, licking his fingers, brushing
them off on his pants—could cover up a spitter without
much trouble. The trick is to get yourself a good habit, a
particular motion or fidget, and do it as often as possible.
Then when you do load one up, your habit will hide it.

I used to lick my fingers a lot (hell, I did everything
but suck my thumb!), wipe them across my letters, do it
again, then wipe them on the front of my pants. Or else
I'd wipe a good honk of sweat off my brow and then make
believe I was wiping it off my pants. It's pretty easy to get
away with a spitter. I don't know whether he does, but
Burdette could throw a spitter all day long and they'd
never catch him, because he goes through the same routine with every pitch. The ump has to catch a guy before
the ball is thrown, or else that damp spot on the ball becomes merely the place where the catcher had spit into his
glove.

Who *me* throw a spitter? Aw, *c'mon,* Ump!

A lot of people ask whether you think about the past
season much during the winter months. My reply usually
is: "Who the hell wants to think about a season like that?"

When a guy has a 5–9 year, and two of the five wins were accidental, he doesn't try to remember it. He doesn't go over each game in his head, as some baseball romantics would have you believe.

I'd forgotten the season by the time my suitcase was packed. In fact, when I boarded the bus to the nearest airport, I'd forgotten my suitcase.

The thing is, you always have the feeling they're going to call you back. Everyone's got a little egotism in him, and I was first in line when they handed it out. (Sometime synonym: *confidence*.) In my case, I always just *knew* that contract was going to be in the mails come January or so. A team doesn't invest a lot of loot in a young kid and then can him after a 5–9 season, especially when that season is his first in pro ball. It's axiomatic in baseball, general managers at contract time notwithstanding, that a won-lost record tells absolutely nothing about a pitcher's performance over the year. For example, that 5–9 record in '56 tells nothing to a general manager about what lousy coaching I'd had, about how Eddie Miller straightened me out, or how I came on like gangbusters at the end of the season.

The smart baseball man—the *fair* general manager—will look at a pitcher's ERA to tell how good or bad he was. A 20-game winner could have an ERA of 6.5, but could be on a team with eight Willy Mayses behind him. A 20-game loser, on the other hand, could have an ERA of 2.0 but have eight Kim Novaks in the lineup. Who's the better pitcher? If a team doesn't score runs for him, the greatest pitcher in the world won't win 20 games.

Listen to me. I got bombed so bad my team could have scored a run a minute and still lost. Ah, but I *finished* strong.

That's the feeling I had when I spent that first off season working for my dad. I know there are a lot of guys who spend only one year in the minors and then go on up to the Biggies. But those are the guys who look like they have all the tools and come along great their first year. They pass the test when the organization gives them a crack at it. They're naturals, in other words.

It's that way in any endeavor, really. If two guys want to be race drivers, for instance, one might have the natural touch and go right on to make it, while the other buckles down to a few years of struggling. Writers, artists, ballplayers—everybody. Sell a first novel, or get ten years' worth of rejection slips. Sell a few paintings and get commissions, or store them up in the garage while you break your neck for an exhibit. Compile a 1.80 ERA in Triple-A ball, or spend a few years playing A to D ball and living like a caveman. May as well flip a coin, really. Me, I'm still flipping.

Of course, it's nice thinking this way now. Nice and mature, right? But in '56, I thought *I* was going to be in the majors in a year or two. And I was damned disappointed when I finally resigned myself to the fact that I wasn't Sandy Koufax.

(By the way, whenever I try to think of an example like that—an example of a once-in-a-decade baseball phenomenon—I'll say Sandy Koufax. I'm not getting any dough for plugging him, honest. He's just the greatest pitcher in organized baseball, that's all.)

Another thing I'm asked about a lot is what makes a good coach and a bad coach. In other words, there I was a green rookie, getting coached like hell everywhere I turned (in most cases)—did I know good coaching from bad coaching, and whose advice did I take when there were two conflicting ideas on how to do something?

The answer lies in the story about my Mattoon days, versus what happened when I went to Tifton with Eddie Miller. Some guys try to coach you—really try, I mean—but they just don't know pitching. Vinnie Zintera was a helluva guy and a good player in his day, but Vinnie knew nothing about how to correct a pitcher's delivery.

Some other guys, though, will know what they're talking about when it comes to pitching. Like Eddie Miller, or some guys who were great pitchers in their own right —a Whitlow Wyatt or a Bucky Walters. Those men would criticize you or give you a tip and it would sink right in. You'd say to yourself, "Jeez, here's *Wyatt* telling me what to do and if *he* doesn't know, nobody does!"

I worked under a pitching coach named Bill Fosdell, on the other hand, who never did a thing to help me as far as I'm concerned. From what I could determine, all he did was sit in the bullpen and keep track of pitchers during ball games. Nothing against him of course, but what kind of coaching is that? Ever try to learn how to dance when you and your instructor are in different rooms?

If you asked Wyatt, he'd stay out on the ball field all

night helping you. He'd go without food or sleep, if he had to, but by God he was there to coach pitching and that's exactly what he did almost every second he was awake. Guys like Walters and Wyatt, I'm sure, have it made as far as money's concerned. With investments and pensions, etc., it's a cinch those guys don't *have* to work. But some guys love the game that much, and all they want to do is help young kids get from the game what they did. Other guys were just putting in their time, collecting their dough and going home every night. The hell with what's-his-name's pitching problems. See you in the morning, Kettle.

The upshot of all this, as far as the minor leaguer is concerned, is that you can spot the "yes-men" right off and determine the guys who are really trying to help. So naturally, then, when the "yes-men" told you something it rolled off you like water from a duck. But when guys like Wyatt told you something, you worked your ass off trying to get it down pat.

So that first year was pretty bad. True, I was old enough to buy a few beers once in a while and generally drown my sorrows, or I could take out a few girls and try to forget getting bombed, but the overall year was a disheartening one. We didn't even have much fun, really. Not like the wild times we had later on, anyway. Nothing funny happened all year, as a matter of fact, unless you think that folding chair in Mattoon was funny. I didn't. I've seen funnier things at wakes.

The only tension-breaker I ran across all season was a

colored clubhouse guy we had at Tifton, whom we called Preacher. Two guys from Alabama, Bud Willis and Bobby Hunt, used to bug Preacher a lot. They'd go out 'gator hunting once in a while, and they'd always bring back something for old Preacher.

One time, they brought him a water moccasin. Preacher, understand, was also a victim of the crummy conditions in minor league ball. Besides having to wash our clothes and polish our shoes, Preacher had to double as groundkeeper and general handyman; he'd be the one who had to do jobs such as chalk the foul lines before a game or patch up the broken-down outfield fences.

One night before a ball game, Willis brought in a dead water moccasin and left it lying around the clubhouse. Fred Hopke, our first baseman and a generally wild guy, put the snake in Preacher's bag.

The last time we saw him after he opened his bag that night, he was climbing the center field fence and going like hell. Preach was scared out of his wits and we all got a chuckle out of it.

I don't suppose it looked too funny, though, when at game time three or four ballplayers in full uniform were laying out the field with cans of lime. I guess we looked like something out of Olsen and Johnson.

See what we had to do for laughs?

Things did get pretty light at Tifton, now that I remember the end of the season. We had come from something like nineteen games behind when I joined the club to finishing only two behind at the wire. During the climb, everyone felt pretty good. You always feel good when you're winning, no matter what the standings are, and when you're climbing toward first place in steady fashion, you always feel a lot better than you otherwise would.

So there were always little tricks we'd play on each other, just out of giddiness. Like nailing a guy's shoes to the floor or switching lockers so that two players would be putting on each other's uniform without realizing it until it was almost game time. Usually this latter happened when two guys showed up late in the clubhouse. They'd dress in a hurry, dash out onto the field, then make two quick U-turns back to the clubhouse to exchange uniforms. We'd laugh like hell from the field. The pitchers who were winning, that is.

So that's the way '56 was. No hits, no runs, no errors. Some day I'll set down how it *should* have been. Whoever coined that old phrase was wrong. It's not how you played the game that counts, it's whether you win or lose.

4

The Greatest Slider of Them All

My contract came in January and it had the exact same terms. It was, again, a contract for B ball. I signed it right away, because I hadn't anything to bargain with. Finishing strong with Tifton in '56 was something, but the rest of '56 made it look pretty scrawny.

Usually a player can send the contract back unsigned, asking for a raise. The thing to do is ask for more than you want, hoping for some kind of compromise at a price close to what you'd like. I pulled this routine later on and it worked, but in '57 I signed and was glad. The fact that I could write my name was all I had going for me.

The thing called for my starting off again in rookie school at Clearwater, Florida. My second race was about to start.

There was one small change in the contract: while it called for B ball, there was no more Wilson, South Carolina team, so we were to play with Hipoint-Thomasville, same state, same league, same class, but a new location with a new franchise. I didn't mind, though. I just wanted to play ball and didn't care if we had to play in Tierra del Fuego. I was anxious to try out my new delivery, à la Eddie Miller, to see if it would carry me through a winning season.

I was kind of cocky when I reported to rookie school that year. After all, I was a man of the world, nineteen years old, and had kept in pretty decent shape playing semi-pro ball Saturdays and Sundays during the off season.

Right off, Don Cardwell, who's now with the Pittsburgh organization, gave me the nickname "Hub" Kettle, after a baseball manager of a few years back named Hub Kittle. Right away I was one of the boys. There were familiar faces and we went out more in the evenings that spring, having a lot more fun than rookie school the previous year. We all had a full season under our belts and the depressing times of the previous year were either forgotten or, in the case of those who had good years, didn't matter. The time was now.

It was different, somehow. Nobody called us "rookie" anymore and we all seemed to acquire nicknames. My old buddy Dick Harris was now "Ricky" for some reason, and Dallas Green was now "Paws." Bob Milo, another pitcher, was now "Mitts." Dallas usually called me "Hands." Don't ask me why. We all felt good, that's all.

It was all more social, like. Even some of the girls we knew were still single. It was going to be a great year.

In fact, it *was* a great year. Mayo Smith was managing the Phillies then, and one day after working out I was called over to the bench where Mayo and Eddie Miller asked me to stay over after rookie school and work out with the Phils. I was delirious. I pitched batting practice mostly, but it was good work and I thought I did very well.

Then I went over to Hipoint-Thomasville (the Hi-Toms) and worked an 11–4 year, with a 3.50 ERA—pretty respectable. I stayed out of trouble on the field that year, too. I threw strikes, had good control and Wyatt was working with me. We had a real good ball club at Hipoint and I guess the better support also contributed to my good year. The weeks training with the Phils also helped my mental attitude a great deal. I mean, after Mattoon I was ready for a starring role in *Breaking Point.*

We moved into the Fort Harrison Hotel with the Phillies, got breakfasts and lunch, and had $67 a week to boot, thanks to Paul Owens and Frank Lucchesi's griping on our behalf for equal entertainment money. We used it mostly for dinners, laundry, etc., and blew the rest at dog races, jai alai games, girls and an occasional movie. Yessir, it sure makes you feel better in the head. The money, I mean.

I roomed with Dallas Green, whom I'd known from the year before at Salt Lake City, and we became close friends. Dallas is one of the greatest guys in the world. He likes to kid around, takes most things with a grain of salt, but he plays his heart out and hates nothing in the world worse than losing. If Dallas thought he could get away with it, he'd hire someone to kidnap the other team, just to win a game by forfeit. I've never played with anyone who played so hard. Maybe if I'd had some of Dallas's drive I'd be up there with him right now. Hang in there, Greenie!

Dallas and I would sit around at night often, or be out sudsing it up, just talking about baseball. We'd gossip about players and managers and generally help each other along with our confident outlooks. Occasionally we'd tip each other off on some trouble one of us was having. I'd come in and ask him what I was doing wrong today, and after he was through ribbing me ("The first thing you did wrong was suit up, Hub") he'd give me some pointers or clue me in on some tip he'd picked up. Dallas was always a better pitcher than I, which is why I'm sitting here reminiscing and he's out there helping the Phils win a pennant.

At Hipoint, we tied for the pennant and lost a seven-game playoff in the seventh game. Not bad, eh? That year had lots of highlights, and tying for the pennant was only one. For instance, that was the year the Russians put up their Sputnik, wasn't it?

The first thing that comes to mind when I think of '57 is the time my folks came back east to watch me pitch a game. I pitched over at Winston-Salem, the Cards' team, about 20 miles from Hipoint. I had a shutout going for 7 innings and really looked good. We beat the Cards 12–2

(Milton K. Bell)

Wearing a Phillies uniform, they say, does something for a young pitcher's ego. In this shot I think I was trying to figure out my new Ego Pitch, which consists of throwing the ball belt-high over the plate at exactly the same instant the batter is in the power of his swing. It works wonders when you're dying for a shower.

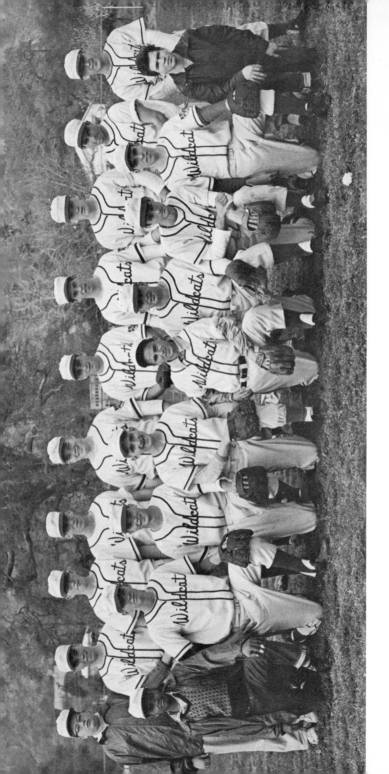

The Monrovia-Duarte High School Wildcats. Chief Wildcat in front, second from left. The "M" on the hillside stands for Monrovia; the "M" in "Miserable" stands for Mattoon.

(Provinzano Studio, Mattoon)

When in Mattoon, and very young, *act casual*.

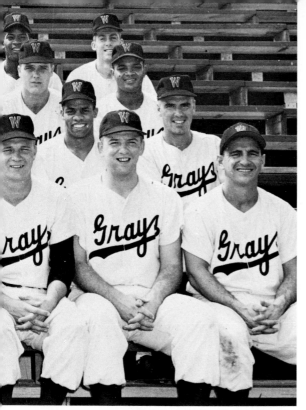

ABOVE: Williamsport '60 championship team. That's Frank Lucchesi in the center. In second row, from left: Pete Cera, Lee Elia, Gordy Figard, me and Dick Harris. Dallas Green had chickened out and went up to the majors.

BELOW: Same Williamsport '60 champs, striking typical minor league attitudes for oficial team photo.

(Williamsport Sun-Gazette Photo)

With Hipoint-Thomasville in '57. Dallas Green, Bob Milo and me. In order of ability.

(John T. Moseley, Shreveport Times)

This is either the Chattanooga '61 team after clinching the pennant in Shreveport or a group of Edsel designers. Me and Lucchesi in front, hamming it up with an eye toward Falstaff Beer endorsements.

Wanderings of a Minor Leaguer.

TOP LEFT: The Last of the Mohicans, Indianapolis '60 version.
(Norman M. Paulson)

TOP RIGHT: Chattanooga, '61. The smirk is because I'm holding a parakeet in my right hand. Or maybe it was a jar of mustard.

BOTTOM: Williamsport, '60. Note roaring crowd in background. Being a hero is hell.

and I felt like King Kong (or Sandy Koufax). That was one of the few times my folks had ever seen me pitch. They never saw me play in high school and rarely came to any of the semi-pro games. A very large thrill, believe me. I remember joking with my dad and telling him I could get him a job as bat boy. I don't think he appreciated my humor, though. Maybe that was why I had my hands full of manure the other day when Dallas called.

What may have helped a lot this year was facing some major league hitters in spring training. The Phillies, in inter-squad games, would send up against me guys like Stan Lopata, Wally Post, Granny Hamner, Richie Ashburn and Del Ennis—most of them old Whiz Kids.

Facing major league hitting for the first time isn't what everyone thinks it is to a young kid. We didn't cringe in fear or wonder how we'd get them out, or any of that stuff. You're built up so high and you feel so good as a result of all this excellent training and coaching (in Phillies' spring training, I mean), that you really think you have it all over them. Also, these are the guys you really bear down against, because if you get *them* out it makes you look that much better.

In spring training, it's the unknowns who give you all the trouble. While the big leaguers usually take it easy and work themselves into gradual shape—oh, the lessons of experience—the unknowns are really trying to make a name for themselves by whacking the hell out of the ball every time up. The young kids are trying to make the ball club; the big leaguers know they've made it. So the kids are knocking themselves out trying to bomb you and the major league batters are taking it semi-easy, just trying to meet the ball and get their eyes. They aren't lackadaisical, of course, but they've been around a while and know how to get into shape. Take your cuts, meet the ball. Take your cuts, meet the ball. The kids, meanwhile, are sliding into first, trying for the fences with every swing, and if they could do it they'd try to bounce a few off your jock just to get on base.

But facing the big boys still does something for your ego, even if you know all this. And it helps to remember striking out Del Ennis twice, say, when you're down in B ball and in a jam.

One day I was introduced to chewing tobacco. Seems like everyone did it, and they figured ol' Hub was about ripe. I had a huge wad of it, and was shagging flies in the outfield and must have swallowed some. About fifteen minutes later I was leaning against the right field fence heaving my guts out. I was *dying!*

They carried me into the clubhouse—also good for a guy's ego!—and were all laughing like hell when they laid me on a rubbing table. I was really hurting. Dallas wanted to give me more, but he was outvoted and I finally was made to drink some Pepto-Bismol, or something equally gruesome. In a few minutes (hours?) I did feel a little better.

Then they went out and got some barefooted kid, about eight years old or so, who always hung around the ball park. They gave this kid some chewing tobacco, brought him into the clubhouse and showed him to me. I got sick all over again. This *baby* was chewing it, but the big bad baseball player was in a semi-coma on the clubhouse rubbing table. Yessir, baseball was starting to be fun.

It really was. One time that year it was raining like hell and the water was three inches deep all around the infield. They had to wait until at least a half hour before game time before they could call a game, but we knew by the time we were suited up that the rain wasn't going to stop and the game would be called.

I was looking out of our dugout, which was on the first base side, toward the stands in back of third. I noticed there were only about three people in the park. It was raining so hard nobody was showing up. I came up with a brilliant idea: I asked the guys how much they'd give me if I ran, fully uniformed, across the field and slid into second as hard as I could. You should have heard them howl.

"No kidding," I said. "I'll do it if you guys'll make it worth my while."

It was about half a second before Dick Harris had a cigar box in his hand and was going around to each guy collecting money. He'd sing out at each stop, "Money for Hub's big slide, folks. Kick in now, and see the greatest slider of them all show his stuff!" They each ran to the dugout, peered out at the rain coming down like crazy and the three-inch puddles all over the infield, and flipped coins into Dick's cigar box. He collected over eight bucks.

I jumped up and ran through the clubhouse and out

onto the field before they had a chance to change their minds. Eight bucks is eight bucks, after all. The rain pelted my face and I ran like mad. About twenty feet in front of second I started into a beautiful hook slide, and mud and water splattered like hell. It flew all over the place in a magnificent spray and splash, and I guess by the time I'd stopped skidding it must have looked like an Iwo Jima landing. Beautiful slide. Kind of fun, too. Try it sometime.

I heard the guys yelling and screaming at me to try the same thing at third, too, but I decided not to and began running back to the dugout. As I turned around and wiped the mud from my face, I saw about 300 fans huddled under the roof behind *our* dugout, waiting to see if the game would be played. You should have heard those people! They hooted and yelled like nothing I'd ever heard before, while I suddenly felt like a naked man at a Solemn High Mass. I still can't figure out how all those people got over behind our dugout—I was *sure* the place was empty.

Anyway, some of them cheered the biggest nut of the century and wanted me to do the same thing at first base on my way in. But I couldn't get back to the dugout fast enough. Dallas had written APPLAUSE in black shoe polish on a towel, and was holding it up to the stands as I came in.

I felt like such an idiot I collected my eight bucks and bought a couple of cases of beer for the guys. After one year, it sure makes a difference, all right.

You know how you hear about guys who do weird

things whenever they've had a bad day? We had a guy like that. He was our center fielder that year, Freddie Van Dusen, who was a terrific ballplayer and a great prospect for the Phils. Freddie was the team's power hitter, consistently up around .330 or so. Whenever Freddie had a bad night, he'd go climb a water tower.

About a hundred feet behind the right field fence at Finch Field was a very high water tower. We'd leave the clubhouse after a bad night and, sure enough, there would be Freddie's car at the bottom of the tower. He'd just go up there and sit, and none of us ever figured out what he was thinking about.

I don't know why I agreed to it, but one night Freddie talked me into going with him. I guess I had just gotten bombed or something, and would have tried anything to straighten out. But there we were, on top of this water tower, and it was scary as hell. I'd never done anything more dangerous than blowing my nose, so it was a brand-new experience for me.

The wind was blowing like crazy and I swear the thing was swaying. Things looked so weird up there, at about eleven o'clock at night, that I was considering becoming a first baseman. I finally said to Freddie, "Okay, Fred baby, we're at the top so let's get the hell down, huh?"

"No, wait a minute," says Freddie. "We're going to walk around the tank first." There was a huge globe tank set on the tower platform, with a sort of catwalk around it. Freddie wanted to walk *around* the goddam thing.

So we started around this globe and all we could hear was the wind whistling around us. Otherwise, it was deathly quiet and more than a little gloomy. Not a sound, except for the wind's steady *whirr-r-r-r*. We got about halfway around the dumb globe and suddenly a flock of pigeons leapt out with the damnedest racket you ever heard. The cold quiet was broken by this God-awful screeching and fluttering and I think I jumped two feet off the catwalk. I thought I'd have a heart attack on the spot. How would you like something like this on your gravestone: *Here lies so-and-so—killed by a flock of pigeons on a water tower after giving up three runs in the ninth inning?* Lucid, eh?

I got off the water tower, drove home, and didn't say a word for two days.

That's the kind of year it was and the mood we were in while heading for the pennant. Frank Lucchesi was managing, having been promoted up from Salt Lake City (you can't get *demoted* from Salt Lake City, unless they send you to Mattoon!), and Frank, besides being a *good* manager, is nevertheless a loose one. He wasn't very strict when we were winning, as we were that year, so everyone could do almost whatever he pleased.

Some of us were boarding with one of the local towns-folk, who'd always offer the club some rooms for the ballplayers. Six of us were staying in adjacent homes, four in one and two in another. One time we were playing ball on one of the front lawns with a ping-pong ball and a rolled-up newspaper for a bat. Our own little game. Next thing we knew some neighborhood kids were joining in, and we developed a pretty good game on this guy's front lawn. The only thing was, we were chewing up the grass something terrible. Seems the neighborhood kids liked to slide a lot.

The owner finally came out and said he was going to throw us out of the house because he'd noticed his lawn was starting to look like the Mojave Desert. We all went upstairs, after trying to console him, to pack our bags and start looking for another place to stay. But the guy came up a few minutes later and told us to forget it, he'd fix up the lawn. We didn't blame him, though. Here was a bunch of pro ballplayers, playing a ping-pong ball game on his front lawn with the neighborhood kids, wrecking hell out of his landscape.

Dallas and I took up a collection and bought the guy some plants and grass seed. If I ever get going well at my dad's nursery, I think I'll send him something for his front lawn.

People were like that in some of the towns we played in. In the first place, they were nice to offer to board the players, but lots of times you'd be shopping in a men's store and the owner would come over and give you a free shirt, or maybe charge you only a buck for a nice pair of slacks. They liked the ballplayers and were proud of the team. Maybe this had something to do with the good year we were having, but little did the good folks know we were just a bunch of kids off the diamond.

Don't believe it? One night we decided to play commando. Yeah, commando, that's right. It was a very warm evening and there was an Olympic-sized swimming pool at a public plunge not far away. Only trouble was, the place had a big fence around it, so who else but commandos could penetrate it? All of a sudden it was Cassino and we had to knock out that Kraut pillbox.

Here was a bunch of us, about two o'clock in the morning and fortified with a few cases of beer, crawling through the grass toward the deserted Kraut pil—er, swimming pool. We knew there was a night watchman, so it was a slow but stealthy group advancing toward the plunge. We crept up to the fence and made it over with no trouble. Quiet as mice. No one said anything to the others, not even a whisper. We dared not arouse the Nazi guard.

We slid softly into the shallow end of the pool and started walking ever so quietly toward the deeper part. You could hear a pin drop and we had really outfoxed the watchman. We were the quietest bunch of raiders in the history of military tactics.

We were swimming around quietly for a few minutes, when all of a sudden we heard a weird whooshing sound, followed by a loud splash. Over and over, real fast. *Whooo-ooo-ooo-oosh*, splash! *Whooo-ooo-ooo-oosh*, splash!

We looked up and here were Dick Harris and Dallas Green beside about five stacks of inner tubes, scaling them down at us. They were *bombing* us!

In about ten seconds all you could hear were guys screaming and yelling and laughing and splashing to beat the band. After all our quiet and brilliant maneuvering to get into the joint, here were half a dozen guys having inner tube fights and making more noise than the entire pool crowd made at high noon. Before we knew it, we were starting off the high-dive board, having a whale of a time. I was about halfway up the ladder when someone yelled, "Here comes the nightwatchman." Then we saw headlights approaching outside.

I jumped off the board, such a brilliant athlete am I, and landed askew on the edge of a concrete layer of blocks set as coping around the ladder-bottom area. Brilliant leap. Twisted both ankles pretty badly. At the time I thought they were both broken, because I could hardly walk. And when it came to climbing the fence when we were trying to get out of there before the guard came in, I was out of it.

So we had a typical battle scene. Here were three guys lifting me over the fence—dragging off the wounded. I don't know how we made it back, but we did. The dirty Krauts had routed our patrol. I was awarded the Purple Heart, with both ankles packed in ice by Dallas and Dick, and we gave Dallas the D.S.C. for piggybacking me away from the scene. Heroes at last.

Next day on the ball field, I managed to fake it. Thank God, I didn't have to pitch that day or I would have been back in Mattoon so fast you wouldn't believe it. I could just see myself explaining to Lucchesi that I'd sprained both ankles leaping off a high board at the city plunge at two o'clock in the morning. I think he would have believed the Cassino story first. Our trainer, Pete Cera, bandaged me up pretty well and I managed not to lose a pitching turn. Wouldn't that have been a great way to bow out?

We were undaunted, though. During the following

week, Dallas and I each pitched a real good game, so just for our own morale we decided to form another commando group. We would take the country club, this time, which also had a large pool and a large fence. The fence here, however, was almost impregnable and for a while we couldn't figure out how to penetrate it. The country club was a quiet place, situated in the middle of a large meadow, adjacent to a golf course. Some day they'll build a cemetery there.

We pulled up in our cars and placed two jacks about three feet apart under the fence. It worked. The fence tore right out of the ground, enough so that we could crawl under it. Only thing that ruined this strategy was the loud *clang-ang-ang-annnnng!* echoing all over the valley.

In the pool, which was smaller than the last one, we started playing water tag. Harris, at one point, was floating on his back at one end in one of the shadows. It was dark and guys could hide out along the edges of the pool if they kept very still. We were looking for Harris, because he hadn't been "it" yet, and Dallas spotted him floating in the water near one edge.

So Dallas, a professional ballplayer like the rest of us, started running down the side of the pool, along the coping, screaming like a banshee, "I got ya, Harris! I got ya!" And he leaps into the pool, the way you would when you just want to land alongside someone and splash hell out of him, sailing through the air with his battle cry on his lips. The publisher won't let me tell you what his battle cry was.

Harris was floating in the wading end, where it was only two feet deep. That's why I can't tell you what Dallas's battle cry was. He must have stove his legs right up through his jaw. I think they shrank about three inches. He couldn't walk for hours, and we once again thought a great pitching career had come to an end, not to mention a great catching career when Dallas finally *did* catch Harris.

So there we were, a week later, carrying out more wounded, dragging him out under the fence and jacking it down in one helluva hurry. It's a good thing none of us *were* in the war. We'd all be speaking German now.

So we tore up the city and ourselves, as well as the league. What a year!

There are sad stories, too, of course. Most of them are too depressing to go into, but one in particular comes to mind which is indicative of one of the many just-plain-rotten breaks that come along. I'm trying to keep this light and airy, which is what baseball essentially is (if there's anything I can't stand, it's a *serious* baseball book), but this story is worth mentioning.

Freddie Van Dusen, when he wasn't sitting on the water tower, was pounding the ball all over the place. He was going great guns, hitting about .350, when a bit of bad luck almost ruined his career.

About six or seven of us were coming out of a bar one evening, when we ran into Freddie cruising by in his car, a brand-new Olds convertible he was really proud of. He was on his way to a hamburger stand about two blocks away to get something to eat. We gave him our orders and decided to wait there for him and try to sober up a bit.

Just before he took off, a couple of wise guys drove by real fast and threw a bottle of beer from their car into Freddie's. Beer splattered all over and Freddie got madder than hell. The wise guys pulled up about a hundred yards down the street and Freddie took out after them, leaving us standing at the curb. One of the punks said something particularly irritating when Freddie got there, and as Freddie reached in to grab him and get a good poke at his smart kisser the guy on the passenger side slashed him across the knuckles with a knife.

Freddie got thirty stitches on the back of his hand and was out for about a month. We ended up tying for the pennant, remember, and with Freddie in the lineup all the time we certainly would have taken all the marbles. It wasn't Freddie's fault, goddam it, and they never did get the two guys. The club hushed up the incident for some reason, and it was released to the press that Freddie had cut his hand on a piece of glass while boning his bat. (Boning a bat is when you get something like a Coke bottle and rub hell out of the surface of your bat to get it hard and prevent it from splitting.)

Freddie did play ball again, but I don't suppose we'll ever know what the incident did to his career. The whole thing was a shame. Besides the implications to Freddie, who knows what winning the flag that year would have done to any of our careers? Freddie was really knocking the ball around when it happened and we missed his bat the month he was out of the lineup. Goddam shame, I say.

So the Hi-Tom Phillies roared through '57 and Hub

Kettle roared with them. I had good stuff and my control got better as the season progressed. I was still using the fast ball, curve and change-up, and Whitlow Wyatt was working with me. My fast ball was good, but I was throwing it overhand, straight as an arrow. Wyatt and Lucchesi got me to drop down just a little, and roll my wrist a bit. The ball started to sink and although I lost a little on the fast ball, it now moved around a trifle more on the way to the plate. My wildness was partially due to throwing straight overhand, because as I fell off to the left in my follow-through I'd lose control of the ball. I'd always been wild high or outside but now, throwing three-quarter overhand and rolling my wrist, the ball was breaking away from the right-hand hitters and into the lefties, but still staying over the plate.

This had a lot to do with the good season I was having, because I only walked about 45 batters that year, a real small amount for something like 130 innings. I had about 82 strikeouts also, which is nothing spectacular, but the small number of walks is what indicated I was coming along as a pitcher. The 11–4 record and the 3.50 ERA combined with this to make my overall effort a pretty good one.

One other event in '57 added to my maturity. No pitcher is worth his salt unless he's been in a fight on the diamond.

It's funny how baseball players always talk rough-and-tough, and think the same way. They're always going to knock somebody down, or deck someone, or charge somebody, or chew somebody out, or any one of a dozen other ways to show the rest how rough-and-tough you are. This is especially true in the minor leagues, where the ballplayers are constantly trying to prove themselves—what better way to do it than to act tough and be rugged?

One time we were playing the Winston-Salem Cardinals and Gene Oliver, who is now with the Milwaukee Braves, was at bat. Gene was leading the league with 30-something home runs and had been hitting us especially, as if he owned our pitching staff. Dallas Green was pitching for us, which meant two pretty big boys were facing each other whenever Gene came up. Oliver's about 220 and 6'3" or so, and Dallas is about the same weight at 6'5".

So Dallas was going to loosen Oliver up a bit. Not hit him or anything. Just loosen him up. It was a tight game in the late innings and we certainly didn't want Oliver to poke one out or go for extra bases in this stage of the game. Dallas threw a tight one and Oliver went down.

Oliver got up and brushed himself off, thinking nothing of it. Good hitters have to live with this, as I said before. It's part of the game. Harris, who was catching, called for a fast ball next, but it got away from Dallas and Oliver went down again. When he got up this time, though, he motioned out to Dallas to the effect that if another one came at him, by God, he'd let Dallas have it and maybe write "Louisville Slugger" across his forehead.

There were about 1,500 or so fans in the stands, and I just knew that Greenie wouldn't go much for a batter threatening him in front of a crowd like that. Oliver seemed a nice enough chap, but it was just the wrong thing to do, justified as he was. I knew the next pitch would sail right at his head.

Lucchesi knew it too, because right then he told us he wanted everyone off the bench if anything happened and out on the field. This was normal enough advice, but we were in the field and when I looked across at the Cards' dugout and saw a solid wall of white uniforms, I didn't feel too hot. Like we had about nine guys on our bench, being in the field, and what the hell kind of odds were those?

So I got ready, and sure enough Greenie let one go and down went Oliver. Oliver got up and started out for the mound. Lucchesi then gave the Charge and off we went. I looked across as we ran out and saw the wall of white moving toward us, feeling a little like the last man at Dienbienphu. Dallas was just standing on the mound, waiting for Oliver to reach him. Just as Oliver got there, Dallas leaped at him and dove right into his midsection rather than wait for him to throw a punch or skull him with the bat. Good decision, I'd say.

Down they went, and you could almost hear the ground shake when they hit. It's funny how no one ever really gets hurt seriously in these free-for-alls. I think it's primarily because of two reasons: nobody really wants to hurt the other guy, and the thing is usually squared away before any acute animosity builds up. Lucky thing.

So by the time Dallas hit Oliver we were all there and, needless to say, vastly outnumbered. I remember grabbing one of their relief pitchers, who was by now on top of Dallas. Harris had stomped out behind Oliver and had started to grab him when Dallas hit him. When they all went down in a pile, they landed on Harris. When I was grabbing the relief pitcher, Harris was yelling something about his stomach.

I was deciding whether to hit this relief pitcher or just shove him off the pile when someone grabbed me from behind and had one helluva stranglehold on me. Next thing I knew I was lying on the grass, gasping for breath, with about eight or nine guys running all over me like I was a base line.

That's the only dangerous part about those things. While nobody is really trying to kill anyone, there are people running all over the place and a guy lying on the ground is apt to get a faceful of spikes or end up with someone stepping a dent in his jock.

Before it was all over, Dallas and Oliver were thrown out of the game, as well as the two managers and the relief pitcher that I had grabbed. I got off easy; in fact, I derived an actual benefit out of the whole mess.

I was pitching the first game of the next series we opened against the same team and this time 4,000 people turned out to see the fireworks. This was the night I beat them 12–2 with my folks in the stands. I don't think I ever thanked Dallas for boosting the gate for my great game in front of my parents. Made the cheering that much louder, etc., etc.

Thanks, Greenie.

In B ball like that, a manager has about eight or ten pitchers and at least six of them are bound to be young

coming-uppers who have to work often before a manager
or scout can tell what kind of potential they have. So the
manager can't afford to rotate four pitchers regularly, as
they do in the majors, because then he wouldn't be giving the coming-uppers the work and practice they need.
It's a tough job, because someone is constantly P.O.'d at
the manager for not pitching him, or, for that matter,
sometimes *for* pitching him.

I bring this up because I think it's important to understand that this is one thing you can't pin on a manager.
He'll never be so zealous to win a pennant that he'll over-
look the welfare of the young prospects. For instance, if a
kid's hurting, has a sore arm, say, in a crucial series or
game, the manager will go with what he has and not risk
hurting the kid's arm for good. And any time a kid has
a sore arm or something else wrong, he should say so and
be put on the inactive list. Minor league managers are
trying to win pennants more often than not, sure, but
they won't take any chances with the kids while they're
doing it. Lots of money invested in these sore arms, don't
forget.

The normal procedure when a manager has a whole
herd of pitchers is for him to pick three as regular starters
and use three more as the fourth starter (or for doubleheader emergencies), rotating them on that fourth turn.
The rest he'll use for long relief or for a fifth starter or
whatever else he might need. Like someone to run out
for hamburgers.

This goes on for a month or so, maybe six weeks, and
then he'll switch it around again. Everyone usually gets

the same amount of work this way, and the same number of chances to pile up a good record.

If one or two—or all—of his starters in regular slots are having a rough go of it, like losing three or four starts in succession, then the manager will alter the rotation and make one of these guys a long reliefer. Or some similar variation. If something very serious happens, like maybe a starter will have a nervous breakdown and completely crack up and become a raving moron, then the manager will make him a catcher. (Hi, Dick baby!)

Heh, heh. Just kidding. You don't really have to be stupid to be a catcher. But it helps.

It's pretty tough on a manager, though. He has a lot of work to do with the pitchers, mostly because that's the largest single lot he has. And pitchers are probably the most temperamental of all ballplayers. The rosters in the minors aren't so big that a manager would have, say, six outfielders to worry about. Normally he's got two catchers, four infielders, three outfielders, a utility man or two, and pitchers crawling all over the place. I'd hate to be a minor league manager. Now that I think of it, in fact, I'd hate to be a minor league pitcher!

So we won the pennant and got ourselves the loser's share of the playoffs, a whopping $90. A lot of guys went out and bought up land with it, some others ordered fancy cars, and still others invested it. I blew mine on six cases of beer and a new jock. Doesn't seem worth all the work, does it? But there are other rewards. For instance, I had a gorgeous callus on my right heel.

I didn't see much action in the playoffs. I only relieved

in one game, when we were behind 3–0. Didn't give up any runs, but we still lost it, 3–0. The Tigers were playing off with us and they had strong power from the left side, so Lucchesi started out three lefties and used Dallas Green in the fourth. Then he'd come back with the three lefties again. I didn't mind at all not being started, I guess. I had the best record on the club; Bob Milo had an 8–3 and Dallas, although even then looking like a great prospect, was 12–9—he worked a lot of innings. Art Hirst, another leftie, was 15–7.

Here comes another thing people asked me about: this business of whether pitching a leftie against a leftie batter, and vice versa—does it really work or is this something managers pull so they won't look like someone who's just paid to make the dugout look fuller?

Some managers—in the Biggies especially—go for what is called "playing the percentages." The theory here is that a batter hits a pitcher better if the pitcher throws from the opposite side. You'll often see a manager put in a leftie to pitch to a leftie, and the batter will still blast one out of the park. The fans then go nuts, scream for the manager's head, and start the Chant of the Fan: "We need a new manager!"; "Whatinell did he pull out so-and-so for with a 19 and 3 record, the idiot?"; "That bum isn't even hitting his weight so whyinell take out so-and-so?" etc., etc.

The thing is, a left-handed pitcher's best stuff is naturally going to break *away* from a left-handed batter. And a rightie's stuff breaks away from a right-handed batter. When something's breaking *away* from a hitter, he's losing a lot of his pulling power, hence a lot of his ability to belt the long ball. And that's a helluva good way to tame a power hitter. All the great hitters have been pull hitters, with rare exceptions. The guys who pull the ball and get all their weight and swing into it are guys like Williams, Musial, Snider, Kiner. That's one reason.

Another is, when a pitcher gets into a jam he'll throw his best pitch. Nowadays, this is more often than not a real fast slider or a good curve. These two pitches, when thrown properly, look like they're coming right at you when you're batting from the same side as the pitcher's throwing from. Then too, if it's right over the plate and you take a cut at it, it breaks *away* from you and takes away some of that pulling power I was talking about.

But in the first place, when a pitch looks like it's coming right at you, your first tendency is to back away a bit. This is true even for Captain Marvel. And when the batter backs away and *then* decides to swing when he sees the ball breaking, it is also lessening his pulling power because he's not stepping into it as much when he does cut at it. Only the very best hitters in baseball can hang in there until the very last moment before ducking if the pitch *doesn't* break. And if it *does* break, only the very best hitters in baseball will catch it before it gets too far away from their power zone.

Simple, eh? So watch what happens next time I'm managing some little league team and I "play the percentages."

All this is a very long-winded way of saying don't be too hard on a manager if he makes a bad call bringing in another pitcher in a tight situation. All he's doing is remembering that a baseball is a very hard object and betting that the hitter has recently read an article on skull fractures.

Most of the time it works, and he's a genius. When it doesn't he's a bum. When it works, the pitcher is a great reliever. When it doesn't, he should still be in Mattoon or, if you don't wish him *too* ill, Vladivostok.

But the percentages show that the odds are with him. You wouldn't bet on heads if the odds were 6–5 tails would come up, would you?

Oh, it's great being an expert, and by the time '57 was over, I *was* one. What a year! Move over, Sandy.

5

⚾

10-5 and Chickenpox

In January of '58 I was chomping at the bit for my contract to come. Just turning twenty that month, I was the Grand Old Man of baseball and I knew I could tear up the league when I got back into play.

When the contract came it said $450 a month, a hundred-dollar raise. A hundred-dollar raise!! For *me!!*

I sent the contract back.

There's something to say about this part of the game. Sort of a game within a game, you might say. After a year or two in pro ball, you never sign a contract right off unless you looked like Grandma Moses the previous season. The game goes like this:

The club sends you a contract, calling for a certain amount of money, say X dollars. You then send it back, without even the courtesy of a letter telling them why you're not signing it. They know why.

Then they send it back to you again in a week or so—if you're lucky—and include a nice little note saying, in effect, "Oh, come on now, son. That's a helluva lot of dough . . . for *you!*"

Then you send it back to them again, this time including a letter telling the club how great you were the previous season, how many games you won, and what an asset you'll be to the club.

Then they send it back to you—if you're lucky—and their letter says how not-so-great you were the previous season, how many games you *lost,* and how they have some doubts about just how *much* of an asset you'll be.

Then you sign and spend the rest of the season putting Band-Aids on your ego. And your wallet.

But this isn't exactly the way it went in '58. Sometimes you've been playing ball for quite a while before you get around to actually signing the thing. And '58 was to be the year I'd receive one of my greatest disappointments, even though having a good year, and the strength of this disappointment, paradoxically, was probably the reason I was to get a concession from the club on my contract disagreement.

Joe Garagiola was only off a few degrees when he said baseball was a funny game. It's a hysterical game.

I was invited to rookie school again. My contract called for a promotion to A ball with Williamsport, Pennsylvania. I was looking forward to playing and was very cheerful about going back to rookie school. The old gang from the previous year was there, including Art Mahaffey, Dallas Green, Dick Harris, Bob Milo and the rest. We worked out according to the same old routine and exercise schedules, and I got myself into pretty good shape.

Then, miracle of miracles, I was asked once again to stay over with the Phillies in spring training and work out with the Big Boys. I worked out well in inter-squad games and I ended up with a pretty good spring training record and all the bigwigs smiling and patting my head more often than usual.

But I still hadn't received the contract back.

I was sent over to Miami again, to work out with that team in Key West. Triple-A ball! Next stop: *stardom!*

This was the year I met some more real fine baseball men, men like Kerby Farrel, an ex-first baseman for Cleveland who managed the Miami team, and Bucky Walters, who helped me a lot and built up my confidence tremendously. I pitched excellent ball with Miami.

In one game, we played Montreal, the Dodger Triple-A team, and I pitched five innings of three-hit ball. I shared the game with Bubba Church, who went the other four. Bob Milo came in briefly in the fifth, but was belted for five runs, so they brought in Church. We lost the game, which was the spring debut, 6–1, but both Bubba and I did well and everyone was pleased with us. I got an enormous thrill sharing the plaudits with Bubba that day; he was a great Philly pitcher in his day.

Incidentally, we had another great pitcher on the roster then. His name was Satchel Paige, and he said he was twenty-nine years old. I remember when he first reported he looked around at the lot of us and asked which one was the bat boy.

Satch was so good with his control, he wouldn't even use the plate to warm up. He'd put a gum wrapper on the ground and, so help me, he'd try to catch the corners! One time (nobody ever believes this) Satch and I were sitting around the clubhouse just waiting for something to happen—I forget what—and I was pumping him for baseball stories and maybe a tip or two. Suddenly he pointed to a small electrical outlet near the ceiling, across the room, and asked how many times I thought a pitcher could hit it.

Well, said I, carefully gauging the distance and size with my trained and youthful eye, I'd be willing to bet nobody could hit the thing more than one time out of ten. The outlet was about fifty feet away, high up on the wall, and was only about two inches by four inches. You needed a Norden bombsight to hit the thing.

Satch stood up and threw a baseball at it. The little metal plate plinked throughout the room. He caught the rebound and threw the ball again. Again the metal plinked. Again he threw it and again the damn thing plinked. Ol' Satch threw that ball six more times in succession before he missed the outlet. Nine out of ten!

Control? He made my arm feel like a busted Gatling gun.

Spring training with Miami was fabulous. Dallas and I each rotated pitching six innings or so, which indicated we were being lined up for starting assignments with the ball club. Triple-A ball! I was getting more excited with every pitch I threw—a starting assignment with a Triple-A club! I really had my hopes up.

We were staying in beautiful Key West, too. The comparison with C, B and A ball is incredible. Beautiful motels, pools and all. We had all we could eat. We could even have more than one container of milk for lunch! In B and C ball we got a little carton of milk and a sandwich. In Key West, we got chunks of pineapple, soup, bananas, lots of milk or iced tea—it was great living. They were even bringing our lunches to the ball park!

Two days before opening day we returned to Miami and I was raring to go. A large parade was planned and the Mayor of Miami gave a welcome speech when we arrived. They took us right to the clubhouse and issued us uniforms—a ritual which thrills a guy to death. There's nothing like getting your own uniform, with the name of the team on the front and a number—*your* number!—on the back, to prove to you that you're there to stay and By-God-They-Believe-You-Can-Do-It. Photographers took pictures of me and Dallas, fans asked for autographs, and all I could think was: Well now, Kettle. Three years and here you are in Triple-A ball. The Biggies next year, baby!

So there I was walking on that big fat cloud, just *dying* to go out and pitch against somebody. I was almost ready to give a bat to nine Miami citizens and offer them five bucks apiece if they could even testify that they *saw* the ball!

Next thing I knew the Phillies had phoned to say they

were sending down Don Cardwell and Kettle was to be sent to the Williamsport Grays in A ball.

Heartsick isn't the word for it. I felt like the president of A T & T the day they told him all the copper in the world had just melted.

The Phillies told me—the age-old excuse again—they wanted me to get in more pitching than I'd get in International League play, so it was Williamsport for me. Don Cardwell is a helluva nice guy—he's now with the Pirates —but that day I hated Don like the plague. I was mad and disappointed and downright abusive, I guess, to a lot of nice guys.

My contract had come back to me while I was with Miami, and I had sent it back again. I wanted that raise. The contract was the first and foremost thing in my mind on the trip to Williamsport. To make matters worse, the weather in Williamsport was miserable. After Key West, I ran into forty-degree weather. I made up my mind right then to quit the game and go home.

Williamsport was almost deserted. It was still a few days before the start of training and there weren't many guys around yet. So, for the lack of something better to do until I could formally resign and leave for home, I got into one of the crummy old uniforms and went out to the ball park to work out. Don't ask me why. I'd run around a while to try to work up a sweat, although it almost froze on me as soon as it formed. Next day I'd do the same, until the guys started drifting into town, and each day there'd be a few more guys to work out with.

Our manager at Williamsport that year was to be Dick

Carter, a strict type who didn't give the players much time to goof around. Like those commando games at Hi-point were out.

The general manager of the Williamsport Club, J. Roy Clunk (believe it or not!), appeared suddenly one day, my contract in hand. You'd have to see this guy to believe him. I mean, this was a real *clunker!* He wouldn't even talk contract with me. Wouldn't utter a word. He'd ask: "Wanna sign, kid?" and I'd say: "No, not like it is," and he'd shuffle off. Wouldn't even bargain!

A few days later, after we'd started training, Dick Carter came out and asked me what the problem was. I told him about the Miami bizzazz I was given and that I'd been asking for $550 on the contract but the Phillies just seemed to be devoting themselves to the task of screwing Kettle. I told Dick—and I was serious this time—that I thought I'd just pack and go home and forget the whole thing.

Dick asked me to come into the office, and we went to see Clunk. The Clunker came up with a brilliant idea. This has to be the most brilliant idea ever conceived. Clunk asked if I'd settle for $500 and the Phillies would pay my way home when the season was over.

I thought I'd laugh myself sick. Which was a refreshing change, anyway. The plane fare home was $118. They'd been arguing with me all along for a lousy $50 a month, for four months ($200), and now they were offering to pay me $500 and then go the cost of the $118 plane ticket. Since they were giving me a $50 raise (per month) anyway, and wouldn't give me the $550 and make me pay my own plane fare, the Philadelphia Phillies had been haggling over a grand total extra outlay of $82! No wonder they were in last place every year! They probably were finishing in first place but added wrong!

This folksy bit of mathematical philosophy shows you how chintzy a ball club can be. It doesn't matter what the *player* asks for, just as long as you make him take *your* terms. No wonder some clubs are hurting for profits.

I signed. I probably wouldn't have gone home anyway. I was broke.

Ballplayers talk a lot of contract among themselves, and you always kind of know about what the other guys are making. And sometimes it rubs against the grain if you're making less than a guy who had a worse previous year than you. You've had the feeling, I'm sure. In fact, all during this contract bickering, a lot of the guys were bugging me to hold out for more. But I was disgusted over the Cardwell incident and mad at myself for not fighting more or bribing Cardwell or something, so I signed for the Clunker.

So the year began, and it turned out to be a good one. I was together with a lot of the old gang, Van Dusen and Harris and Hopke and Art Hirst and some others, and I wound up the year 10–5—not too bad. The reason it wasn't too bad was because I was out three weeks with the chickenpox! I was even quarantined for 10 days.

Here I was quarantined with chickenpox, having to stay in the apartment while all the other guys could go play ball. All I could do to keep from going nuts was stay there and stare out the window. One time a few gals we knew came over, but all they could do was sit in the parking lot and yell up to the window at me. They brought me model airplanes to build, puzzles, Brenda Starr cut-outs, and all that jazz. Little Jerry would gaze out the window and talk to his little playmates in the parking lot below. It's tough being a professional ball-player, but it's even tougher when you've got the chicken-pox on top of it. Kind of a double disease.

Aside from that, it was a pretty fair year, although the season started off in bad shape when we lost five straight. Then I pitched against Lancaster, the Tiger club, one day when it was raining. We eventually won, 8–4, but you should have heard each side scream their heads off in the proper sequence. Before five innings had passed we were ahead, so the Lancaster bench was riding the umpires to call the game. Since we were ahead, they'd be off the hook if the rain kept up and the game was called. But we, in turn, rushed like crazy through a few innings and after the fifth-inning mark it was our turn to ride the umps to call the game. We were ahead 5–0, so if the umps called it we had it in the bag. So each bench—Lancaster was managed by fiery Johnny Pesky at the time—rode each other and I slipped and slid my way through to the first Grays win of 1958.

I remember it was Bob Rodgers who wrecked my shut-out in the eighth inning. An error, a walk and Rodgers' single broke it, and I got kind of shook up. I didn't get them out until four runs later.

Remember Freddie Van Dusen? Well, I guess that wa-ter tower sit-in payed off because Freddie, about two weeks later, got me my third win with a pinch-hit grand slammer. We were down 3–0 in the late innings and Jose Pagan had been giving me fits all day. I think he had two key doubles off me and Jim Duffalo was keeping us pretty tight in relief. In our half of the eighth inning, I was just sitting in the dugout watching a great game go out the window, damning the crummy park and the rotten infield and wondering where I could get a voodoo doll that looked like Jose Pagan.

But it turned out to be Jose who started us off, putting our first man on base with a throwing error. I wouldn't need the doll after all. I sacrificed the runner along, and Fred Hopke dumped a Texas Leaguer into right field when Ernie Bowman ran smack into Johnny Weekly in the outfield. Somebody then walked, somebody else struck out, and Carter sent in Freddie Van Dusen to pinch-hit when the other manager took out Duffalo and put in Chet Vincent. I remember thinking about Freddie's tough break the previous year, and the situation couldn't have been better planned for Freddie's Great Revenge.

He stroked the first pitch over the right field fence and I almost yelled myself hoarse. We didn't sit on any water towers that evening but I spent a nice piece of change buying Freddie beers for the next week. What a shot!

Playing conditions—again—were pretty bad. We had to shower and change in our hotel most of the time, because the clubhouses looked like Berlin after the war. They were large privys, actually. Not even flushing toilets. All we had was a long trough, with a few boards with holes in them for the other requirements. Most of the time the guys went to the bathroom before they left for the ball park, or else tried to find a semi-hidden bush behind the grandstand. By the time the season was three weeks old, we had a regular list of the best gas stations in town to hit on the way back from the field. And we usually had some kind of pool going as to the exact day the hotel was going to collapse.

We had another fight that year, too. It was the Cards again, but this time with their York, Pennsylvania, team.

We had a catcher named Mack Burke, a $40,000 bonus baby. Mack would get ridden hard whenever things weren't going right—especially since we were having a pretty mediocre season. Bonus babies have a tough go of it in the minors (more on this later) so most of the time they're in a pretty rotten mood. Mack, this year, had to put up with "forty thousand dollars, my ass!" from the crowd whenever the bat boy stubbed his toe. It was conveniently simple for the rest of us, because whenever we lost it was naturally Mack's fault, so it's easy to see why he was in a bad mood this one day when we played York.

Walt Matthews, a York man, tried to score from second on a base hit, but he was out by fifteen feet at home. When Mack tried to tag him, Matthews kicked out with his foot and cut Mack's leg. They bounced away from each other, but it was obvious watching them get up that Burke was going to crush Matthews' skull with his bloody leg.

Bob Milo, who was pitching for us and was backing up the play at the plate, came running over and belted Matthews from his blind side. I mean, he really smashed him—Matthews went down like an abandoned puppet, out like a light.

So here we went again. The charge was sounded and both benches emptied. Almost the same bunch of guys, too. I think the Cards had about six or seven players on their bench who were in the Green-Oliver fight the year before, and our guys were almost the same too, so it was really a rematch.

White and gray suits and arms flying around and sand whizzing past my ears, umpires and managers shouting at each other. Wonderful way to spend a few innings. I remember grabbing one of their outfielders, both of us bouncing and rolling toward the grandstand behind home plate. We wound up with this guy on top of me, but I had his arms locked so he couldn't start reshaping my face. Next time I looked up this other little guy was sitting on top of us, but beating the hell out of the top of my head. I couldn't let go of the guy I had locked up or he'd start his own rapping, so I spent most of the fight trying to duck this little guy who was knocking me right straight on top of the head at about eight blows per minute.

It wasn't until the next day that I found out the little guy was the Cards' fourteen-year-old bat boy they'd brought from York.

After the fight the place was a mess. The outfielder I'd been wrestling with was named Koenig, and we got up and started brushing each other off. He asked if I was okay, and I did the same; nice and friendly-like. Two minutes before, we'd been trying to flatten each other, but now we were the best of friends. I'll never understand it.

Somebody had scratched hell out of Milo's face, just as if a girl had attacked him. His face looked like a railroad siding. Matthews was an absolute wreck. His eyes were black, his cheek was swollen, he had blood all over his tattered shirt and he generally looked like a survivor from Shiloh. In fact, Matthews looked like the way I felt after signing my contract that year.

The season went by pretty fast. I was concentrating on the details of my pitching, a nice change from the year before when I had a great ball team behind me. My speed was up, my stuff would break well, but I developed something that always seemed to throw me off in the late innings. I'd throw a good game, but around the eighth or ninth I'd start walking batters or getting knocked around pretty solidly.

Carter put me over to throwing relief for a while, just so I could keep throwing but not take any undue risks by starting more games in which I'd have to throw very hard for nine innings. I didn't mind, as long as I could pitch. So now I was a long relief man.

The switch was sudden, and it led to a dubious thrill. I became one of that rare breed, that special corps of iron-willed supermen: in one day, a doubleheader with Allentown, I lost the game I started and won the game I relieved.

I started the first game, and was bounced out by the fifth inning. Carter went through his whole staff trying to salvage that one, but we couldn't. In the second game, we found ourselves tied up in the eighth, so Carter called me in and I went the eighth through the eleventh, finally getting the win. I was beginning to believe relieving was where I'd make my greatest contribution to the Phillies' cellar-dwelling organization.

I have to make a confession here. Whenever these little thrills would pop up, like winning and losing a game in a single day, I'd buy about nine copies of the local paper and clip out all my press coverage. If you haven't figured it out by now, though, I'd only send home the good ones. My mom kept a scrapbook, and to look at it today you'd think I was Mandrake the Magician wherever I played. Not a single bad review.

There was one more "first" that year. My first big beef with a manager.

We were playing Redding, the Indians' Club, and I was going pretty good all through the game. In the bottom of the eighth it was 1–1, and I was feeling pretty fine. My stuff was nicking the corners and I could throw the ball wherever I wanted.

The first guy up flew out. The second guy singled. That's okay. Don't worry about him. Hold him on Fred, baby. (Hopke, our first baseman.) Man on, one down. That's not so bad, Kettle, just hold it tight.

The next batter I worked to two balls and one strike. I had beautiful stuff. I was peering in to get Burke's signal when I heard time called and the batter stepped out. I looked around and almost had a heart attack when I noticed Carter walking toward the mound. What in the sweet hell did *he* want?

Carter was too much. I couldn't believe my ears.

"I'm taking you out, Hub." He had his hand out for the ball, but I still couldn't believe it. This was *my* game. One down, man on first, and I'm working a fine game. What was he, some kind of nut?

"Are you shittin' me, Carter?" No kidding, that's what I said. "I can get this guy out. This is my game."

Carter was beautiful. "I know you can, Hub, but I want Milo to pitch to him. I want a left-hander."

This was the first time I'd ever talked like that to a manager. I really couldn't believe what was happening.

"Your ass, Carter. Give me a chance to get him out, willya? This is *my* game." I knew I could do it, too. I've been in trouble before, and this certainly wasn't anything even remotely resembling trouble on the mound. All I wanted was for Carter to have a little guts and leave me in.

He took me out. He took me out of the goddam game, for no reason at all. Here I was a young kid trying to make the big time, needing every win I could get my hands on, and Carter takes a sure win right the hell out from under me. When I reached the dugout, I kicked a trash bucket clear across the bench and got some pretty dirty looks. God, I was mad!

When you're in shape you sweat easily, and I had a good soak on that day. Somebody in the dugout gave me my jacket, and I shouted, "I don't want the goddam thing," and threw it on the ground right in front of Carter. He ignored it completely.

To top it off, Milo threw five straight strikes and retired the Indians, making Carter look like the greatest genius since Ben Franklin, and me look like a punk kid having a cute little tantrum. But dammit, the thing is, Carter took a sure win away from me that day. We scored two runs in our half of the ninth, and the Indians scored one in their half. Milo got himself a beautiful, big, fat WIN on his record, and I got zilch for a great game.

I was storming. Guys were trying to shake my hand for a good effort, but I wouldn't shake with anyone. I banged locker doors, kicked buckets, threw clothes all over the clubhouse. I knew I'd lost the win, and didn't much care how it looked in Carter's report. He may have still raved about me in his weekly report to the Phils on each player, but all I could see was that won-lost record losing a nice fat one.

The next morning I couldn't sleep late, as we usually did, because the phone woke me up about nine o'clock. It was Carter, and he wanted to see me down in the lobby right away.

Carter, in the hot sun outside the lobby and with me still half-asleep, balled me out pretty good. He was nice about it, but he let me know how bush-league it was to talk to a manager that way, and that my attitude wasn't right, and that I acted like a punk kid, and that Milo pitched pretty good, and that I was just being silly about the whole thing. He was right of course, but the funny thing about it was that three weeks before that, I'd been knocked out of the box early and we lost the game, but I was still jolly and horsing around on the bus that night. Carter had told me then that for a guy who had a game to win or lose and blew it, I was certainly happy and I sure had a good attitude and all that jazz. Now, he was telling me how bush I was acting.

I explained to Carter that the last time I'd been pure and simple knocked the hell out of the box. But last night, I told him, I was really fighting it down to the wire and had the game in my pocket, and he takes me out of it. I also explained that while I knew I pulled some pretty childish stunts in the dugout and clubhouse, I talked sanely and sensibly to him on the mound.

Dick's a good guy. We talked it out and nobody was the worse off for it. I even learned a little humility, I guess. On a ball team, you're with the same guys for six months or so, and you get to know everyone pretty well. There are times when a guy won't even spend every day of six months with his wife; imagine what it's like eating, sleeping and traveling with the same nineteen-or-so guys for six months straight.

So you get to be a closely knit group, almost like a family. I've never seen guys kissing up to managers, or any Army-life type of grudging relationships. Everything with the managers and coaches is normally on a pretty friendly and informal basis. Thank God, anyway, because Dick and I patched things up just great. I made Milo buy me plenty of beers for that win, though.

Yessir, '58 was a fine year. When I came back to work in my dad's nursery that winter, I felt pretty good. 11–4 in '57 and 10–5 and chickenpox for '58. I'd even almost forgotten about J. Roy Clunk and that incident with Don Cardwell.

Almost.

6

⊖

A Wing and a Prayer

I started out '59 in the usual manner: bad. I developed arm trouble right off, at the Philly rookie school, and spent most of the season recovering from a lousy start. I wound up 10–10, after losing the first two games at Williamsport, but I pitched a pretty bad year all around. I like to call it "mellowing with age."

The contract that came on my twenty-first birthday called for a crummy $50 raise, to $550, but called for me to play with Buffalo in the International League— Triple-A ball. I felt good about playing there, since it was another step up the ladder and indicated the Phillies were high on me, but the dough was sad. I sent the contract back without looking at it twice. Once again, I went off to rookie school without having signed it.

It was like Old Home Week again. Mahaffey, Green, Keegan, Milo, Harris, Hopke, Van Dusen, Bobby Wine— the whole gang was there again. But the reunion festivities were hardly over when I got inflamed tendons in my right arm and couldn't throw a baseball through a wet Kleenex.

At the end of rookie school I was asked again to stay over and take spring training with the Phillies, but my arm was so sore I only stayed in Clearwater a week before I had to come home and wait it out before reporting to the other club.

I met that brick wall while in Clearwater, though. They gave me a bucket of balls and had me stand fifteen feet away from the center field wall and just throw balls at it. I'd bend down, get the rebound, straighten up, and throw the ball at the wall again. Great fun. I felt like an optimistic East Berliner. The idea was that since my arm was so sore and I couldn't pitch at all, I could still get that small amount of exercise and maybe work out the soreness. Fifteen feet isn't too far, normally, but I got pretty sick of that routine and it wasn't doing my arm one bit of good.

I was also getting heat treatments and whirlpool baths —the whole bit—but my arm still wasn't making it. It was killing me and on a few occasions I even had to *drink* left-handed.

Finally I told them I wanted to go home for the three weeks or so that remained before I was due to report for spring training with Buffalo. I figured if I got a few weeks' rest and then started all over again, it might be better. That way I'd give my arm a chance to heal by itself instead of working it to death in front of a brick wall and dying of pain for three weeks. I still hadn't signed the contract, but I knew Buffalo would be the place I'd be going eventually.

Gene Martin, the Philly farm director, didn't go for the idea at all. We went around and around for a while, and I finally declared that I was going home, period. I explained that I wasn't really supposed to be in Clearwater by then anyway, since most of the other guys not invited had already gone home. The Phils no longer had Mayo Smith; Eddie Sawyer was their new manager and Dick Carter was now a major league coach. I felt that, together with my painful arm troubles, we weren't getting much attention down there anyway. While their letting me stay over to work out my arm was still an honor, I felt the best thing I could do was go home and rest my arm to see whether it would heal.

Martin was pretty upset about my leaving, but I'm sure he wasn't as upset about that as the Phils were about having to pay my way home. After some bickering and haggling, they finally came through and paid $150 to get me back to Monrovia, and then $150 again when I reported to Buffalo. The Phillies sulked for weeks. Seems kind of stupid the way they scream and holler over piddly sums, but then go out and blow a fortune on a bonus baby.

At home, I just rested. I did a little running but didn't work my arm at all, and by the time I reported to the Buffalo training camp in Dunedin, Florida, it was feeling much better, but still hurt some. Every time I tried to throw a ball I couldn't last more than an inning or so before the arm started paining again and I'd have to stop. I wound up not pitching at all in spring training games.

The Phils came through again, though. This was the second time I was with a Triple-A club, and it was the second time they took me off it. They sent me down to Williamsport again—back to A ball. Only this time I didn't blame them. I had a bum arm, and that was that. The Phillies needed me like they needed another last-place season.

From the Buffalo camp I went to Kissimmee, Florida, where the A and B clubs were working out, and it was Old Home Week once again. Everyone had finished with rookie school and Phils training by this time, and most of my buddies were at Kissimmee scrambling around trying to get themselves a niche for the coming season. Some guys, like Green, had chickened out and gone up to Triple-A or the Biggies, but most of us middle-of-the-roaders were still around. It helped take my mind off my fading career, anyway.

First thing I saw when I came to town was Freddie Van Dusen riding down the street like a bat out of hell on a motorcycle. He had told some salesman he was interested in buying one and talked him into a whole day of trying it out. So everyone was already there when I pulled in, and my first greeting was Freddie whipping around like Marlon Brando. I didn't notice, but I suppose there weren't any water towers around.

There was a big lake a block away from this dump we were staying in, a pretty sad joint. Conditions were terrible all around again, anyway, so I suppose this was consistent at least. In our clubhouse we didn't even have lockers. We just strung wires across the room, on which we'd hang our uniforms, jocks, etc. Especially tall guys caught it right around the nose area.

Anyway, this lake was too much of a temptation for our crowd. We all bought fishing gear and would spend most of the time trying to catch something. One day four of us decided to rent a motorboat and go out to the middle for the big ones. Freddie Van Dusen was the sailor in the crowd, and he was elected to man the motor and captain the excursion.

It was Harris, Hopke, Freddie, Bobby Wine and myself. The wind had come up and the waves were higher than usual by the time we pushed off. Bobby Wine decided he'd swamp the boat about halfway out, and each time a large wave came along he'd throw his weight to the front of the boat with a few other guys and we'd get a boatful of water. Hopke couldn't swim and was yelling bloody murder for us to get back to shore. All the while, Freddie was manning the motor, shouting "Mister Christian! Mister Christian!" at Bobby Wine, who in turn was laughing at Hopke's expression every time a wave hit us.

So the boat did get swamped and finally sank. We all leaped out and started swimming for it, with a few guys helping the screaming Hopke. The boat was about three feet under, and Freddie was still sitting by the sputtering motor, in water up to his waist, yelling something about going down with the ship.

We were all swimming like hell and trying to save

Hopke, and we didn't notice that the water was only four feet deep. We could have *walked* to shore.

Van Dusen finally dragged the boat in, turning it over and emptying all the water out. We walked along the shore with the damn thing and turned it in to the guy, looking innocent about his motor being full of water. I still don't know if it ever ran again.

At Williamsport, I was put on the inactive list for about a month after losing my first two starts. I'd been bombed out of both in the early innings. Lucchesi was our manager again, and he ran a good show. We had a fine ball club. When I came off the inactive list Frank played me often and I wound up 10–10—not bad for a comeback but certainly no great shakes. Twenty decisions is a helluva lot, especially after being inactive for a month, but my pitching was terrible. I was hit pretty hard, even while winning, which, in baseball, is a little like having the dentist tell you your teeth are all right but your gums have to come out.

We got into the playoffs that year with the Giants' club, Springfield. The Giants had sent Julio Novarro to Springfield from Phoenix to help the former team clinch the pennant, and Julio came through winning seven games. We finished a game and a half behind them. Julio's now with the Angels.

The best game I pitched all year was in the playoffs. In the first game, I was opposing Julio and had a shutout going for eight innings. But Springfield scored three runs when Matty Alou slammed a homer off me. I struck out eleven and only walked one. Lost it, but it was still a pretty decent game.

1959 was the year Curt Simmons was sent down to the minors by the Phillies. Curt hadn't been throwing too well and the Phils wanted him to get into better shape. He drove down to Williamsport and we'd been told earlier that he was coming. We were getting ready to go on a road trip and this news, to us, was like hearing that Lyndon Johnson was coming over to help with your income tax return.

We got a big rusty spike and banged it into the wall in the clubhouse. We then put a strip of adhesive tape over it and wrote on it as sloppily as we could, SIMMONS. On the spike we hung the rattiest, filthiest, holiest uniform we could dig up.

I'll never forget wondering how he'd react. We were all standing around in denims and wrinkled sport shirts, and Curt came in wearing a neat sport jacket, trim and pressed slacks, and was generally impeccably dressed. When he saw his "locker" he almost split a gut laughing and we were all kind of relieved.

In fact, Curt went downtown the very next day and bought about three pairs of denims and some nondescript sport shirts. Great guy, Curt.

Curt was with us for about a month. When he left us he actually said he'd had a better time with us than he'd ever had in the Biggies, in terms of fun and a gang of guys who were pretty nice to play with on a ball club. I don't recall if any of us actually said it, but I'm sure most of us had a fabulous example to live up to after having known

Curt. A great guy and a great ballplayer. He was another one who'd sit up all night with the kids and talk about their pitching with them. Never a know-it-all, never offering advice unless asked for it, Curt probably did more good on that club for a lot of young guys than an entire staff of coaches and managers could. And he'd always take an active part in our goofing around.

We played cards a lot on long bus trips, and one of the favorite pastimes was kibitzing around trying to make a cardplayer so mad he couldn't think straight enough to win.

One time Curt and I were playing gin rummy on the back seat of a bus. Gordy Figard was sitting next to me, watching the game. I've never played so well before or since, but that night I ginned about eight times in succession and Simmons was starting to get a little P.O.'d. Figard had been taking it all in, and on the next hand he scooted over close to me and whispered into my ear, pointing to a card. I whispered back, just loud enough so Curt could hear, "Yeah, but I don't know about that one, Gordy." Then Figard would whisper some more and Curt would start tapping his fingers trying to be patient.

Then I'd play a card and Curt would follow, but then Gordy and I would start up again. My next card would be a gin and Curt would go wild. Next hand we did the same thing—I'd gin again, and Curt would really burn. Next hand the same, and so on, except that with each successive hand Gordy and I would draw it out longer until eventually Curt would bang on the table and say "C'mon, let's go. Play cards, Jerry!" Then I'd play and gin and Curt would just mumble to himself for five minutes.

We rubbed it in by saying, "Wait a second, Curt, wait a second. This means a lot to us poor guys." Then he'd drum his fingers and whistle and finally say, "Okay, okay. C'mon, c'mon, let's play, huh?" Then I'd gin again.

Finally, when I'd ginned about twelve straight times, an incredible amount, Curt threw the cards down and wouldn't play anymore with Gordy or me. He never knew that the card I threw after talking to Gordy was the card I'd started to play in the first place.

There are always a few funny guys on a ball club. For two years or so I was blessed with Dick Harris and Gordy Figard. One time, we were on a bus on the way to Allentown and started to bug Gordy.

Gordy, as long as I've known him, would never break down and buy a traveling bag. He used to get a regular cardboard box and put two holes in it for handles—this was his traveling case. We'd always wise off at him, just to make the trip shorter, to go-out-and-get-a-goddam-traveling-bag.

"Hey, Gordy, why the hell don't you leave your chickens home and get something to carry your clothes in?"

"Screw you, Kettle."

Somebody else, in the back of the bus: "Figard, I hear you're so cheap you sneak into the ladies' rooms and use the free Lady Elgins."

Me again: "C'mon, Gordy, buy a purse like every other broad."

It went on like this for a few minutes, kidding him about his dumb box of stuff. Next thing, I grabbed his box from the rack and stomped all over it, busting it up completely.

All our clothes and personal stuff was in the bottom of the bus, and our baseball equipment was in the overhead racks. The idea was to grab this stuff first and go right to the ball park, and then unpack the rest when we came back to the hotel. Kind of like a potluck picnic.

It always wound up like a Laurel and Hardy show. I'd do something to Gordy, and he'd turn around and do something to me.

Gordy grabbed my hat from my bag and folded the bill completely in half, and then ripped the hell out of it. Then he jumped up and down on it and made it look like a W. Funny, eh? Then he placed the hat back on top of my bag, delicately, like it was a single rose on a dinner table. Beautiful motion.

By this time, everyone in the bus was yelling, "You gonna let him get away with that, Hub?" Nice guys. They'd do anything to settle an argument.

So I sat there a minute, looking at Gordy, then at my bag, then back at Gordy, all the while hearing the guys laughing like hell and asking me if I was going to let him get away with it.

I took his box, dumped it upside down in the aisle and scattered everything all over the place, and finally ripped his traveling box into tiny shreds of cardboard. Then I threw the pieces out the window and sat down like I was J. Paul Getty.

Then Gordy got up and ripped the bill right off my hat, leaving it hanging by a few threads, just so the bill hung down around my ear when I wore it. He also ripped the seam from the top on down to the front. It kind of looked like a Mickey Mouse hat.

This was all a riot, of course, but I was due to pitch in Allentown that night and we didn't have any extra hats. Do you think *anyone* who wasn't playing would let me use his hat? You're right.

Pete Cera, who was our trainer and one of the funniest guys I've ever met, was faced with me dropping that hat in front of him in the clubhouse that evening, saying, "Okay, Pete, see what you can do with that hat, huh?" I told him otherwise I'd wear a batting helmet for the game. Pete grumbled an okay and I went out to the field wearing a helmet to warm up.

When he brought it out to me, he had put about six stitches in the bill to hold it in one piece, and had secured the bill to the cap itself with white adhesive tape. Tape was also used to hold the seam together. In a fit of artistic frenzy, Pete had painted the tape black with shoe polish so it wouldn't be too obvious what I was playing in. He did a good job, too, since our hats were black with a red-and-white letter in front.

In the fourth inning, after I'd been sweating heavily for some time, I noticed the batters giggling and snickering when they stepped up to the plate. A few times I checked with Harris behind the plate and Hopke at first to find out what the hell they were all laughing at, but both of them just shrugged it off and said the opposing hitters were just trying to rattle me.

But when the fans started laughing, I figured something was wrong, and I finally felt like an idiot when I discovered that my face was covered with black streaks from the shoe polish-sweat combination. I looked like a zebra.

I tried to fake my way through the game, wiping my face often with my arm, but when the sweat finally soaked clear through the hat, the tape gave way and after every pitch my hat would fall into three pieces.

Luckily, I got bombed in the sixth and taken out for relief. I felt like I'd been freed from a zoo. Even Lucchesi was laughing from our dugout, but that was because we were in first place at the time and he always did have a knack for the sport's entertainment value.

Cera, whom I was with from '57 to '60, would get about $3.50 a month from each player as clubhouse dues so that he could buy sweat socks and other miscellaneous items for the team. Riding Pete about this little chore was always good for a laugh.

With a new pair of socks, for instance, we'd whine about one having a hole in it. "Can't wear these, Pete. Look at that hole."

"Holy Jeez!" he'd yell. "Lucchesi, take Kettle out of the lineup. He can't pitch tonight because he has a hole in his sock!" Once in a while he'd change his tack on us:

"Pete, there's a rip in my uniform. Could you patch it up?"

"Too bad," he'd bellow. "You ripped it, you wear it!"

Cleanliness of the uniforms used to really bug Pete. Each time we finished a road trip all our home uniforms were freshly cleaned. I think once a week they'd get a cleaning, whether they needed it or not.

One time when we started a home stand, I went out on the infield with my new clean uniform and rolled around in the dirt until I was filthy dirty. Then I came back into the clubhouse and Pete almost had a stroke when he saw me. Nothing against Pete, of course, but such an idiot act by one of the players made him look bad because it was his job to see that we had clean uniforms. He'd blow his stack.

"Hey Luke, Luke!" he'd call to Lucchesi. "Look what one of your knuckleheads did to his uniform!" He'd yell this while dragging me by the sleeve into Lucchesi's little cubbyhole, where Frank would be sitting in his shorts, smoking a cigar and making out a lineup or something.

"What'd you do, Jerry?"

"Well, I slipped on the infield, Skip. Sorry I messed up the suit."

Then Lucchesi looked at Pete and said, "What are you getting so excited about, Pete?"

Cera would get more livid. "Are you kidding me, Luke? This clown's done it every week for the whole season!"

Then Pete would walk away mad and the whole team would roar. Pete was a grand guy. When we weren't making it impossible for him, he really did take great care of the players and their equipment.

We were on the road playing and we'd been winning and were on top of the world. In the hotel where we were staying they had a big Canadian flag and an American flag still on the flagpole at midnight one night. The pole hung from a second-story window, and we had to walk an eight-inch ledge to get to it.

We hijacked both flags and nailed the Canadian one across Cera's door so he couldn't get in. We did the same to Lucchesi's room with the American flag.

Pete and Frank came back to the hotel about an hour later, after a few beers and a hamburger, and couldn't get into their rooms. They couldn't rip down the flags, of course, so they paid some flunkey to take them down, but made him promise not to tell the hotel manager.

Next morning the manager was yelling at Lucchesi that someone had stolen his flags. Lucchesi was brilliant. "How the hell would *I* know where your goddam flags are?" Then the manager ran down the halls, banging on every player's door trying to find out where his flags were. We'd look at him like he was a nut and threaten to call the hotel manager if he didn't quit bugging us about his flags. The poor guy finally went back downstairs.

The flags were in Cera's closet. That night, about two in the morning, Lucchesi crept into Milo's and my room, asking us if the Human Fly who stole the damn things wouldn't put them back on the pole. Next morning on the bus he collected from us the dough he spent getting the flags off the doors.

One guy, by the way, almost didn't finish out the season. We were finishing up a road trip at Allentown, and a lot of people from Williamsport came down to see the series. One of them was his girl friend, whom he'd been dating all season.

One night they were in his room pretty late, when Lucchesi decided to pull a bed check. When he banged on the guy's door, saying, "Open up, it's the Skip," he and the girl panicked and the girl ended up under the bed. I guess Luke heard the commotion because when he came in and had checked the guy out, he started looking around. He finally spotted the girl under the bed, told her to come out, but she'd be damned if she would. Frank told her he could wait all night if he had to, and sat right down on the bed. The girl still wouldn't budge, and the guy was in a cold sweat. After an hour or so—believe it or not—Lucchesi told the girl she'd won and left. Before leaving, though, he fined the guy $25.

I never found out what the upshot was, if any, but an hour after Lucchesi left, the girl was still under the bed refusing to come out. The guy said she slept under it, leaving only when we'd all gone down to breakfast. Guess she hadn't known many ballplayers.

I became very friendly with Fred Hopke, our first baseman. Fred and I played on the same team for three consecutive years and were in spring training together often.

He was a helluva guy, and could always take a joke—a prime requisite for "helluva guys."

One time we were playing in Reading and were getting ready to leave the dressing room for the game when Gordy Figard came in and announced that he could lift up any three guys off the floor. This was all preplanned, but Hopke wasn't in on it.

We all laughed at Figard, of course, but he insisted he could do it. After egging him on for a few moments, getting Hopke all heated up to see confident Figard pull off this feat, we lay down on the floor, Hopke in the middle and Dick Harris and me flanking him. Hopke tucked one arm under each of us, since he was the one Figard was going to lift. By having Hopke brace Harris and me, Figard would be lifting three guys when he lifted Hopke. To add to the solidarity of the trio, Harris and I each had one leg cocked around Hopke's so we were all one single unit, more or less. Naturally, poor Hopke was pinned and couldn't move a muscle.

Then Figard leaned down, flexing his muscles, and grabbed Hopke by the belt. He opened the belt, undid Hopke's pants, and right on cue Pete Cera walked in and painted Hopke's penis and testicles with black shoe polish. Which is hard to remove, unless you scrub real hard. Which I doubt Hopke did, because he didn't take a shower with the rest of us for a week.

All this fooling around was good, because my pitching needed it. Record-wise, '59 was okay, but that 10–10 didn't really show how badly I was actually doing. I'd always had control problems, but the arm trouble was confounding the issue. There was a stretch there when the local papers were comparing me to Robin Roberts. This is a compliment in any man's book, but the reason they were comparing us is that we each gave up home runs like they were going out of style.

I'd win a ball game 5-1, say, and you could bet Fred Hopke's shoe polish that the 1 was a home run. If I lost a game 5-4, there were usually a few homers in the tally and more often than not, homers with men on base—the ones that *really* hurt.

I've always said, though—and any good pitcher will agree with me—that it's far better to give up a home run once in a while than to give up, say, a couple of singles or walk a few guys. It's when you walk them or give up a few of those little dinky hits that the opposing team usually builds up a big inning. A home run, with nobody on, doesn't really shatter the scoring. Your ego, yes, but not the scoring.

Then too, sometimes a pitcher uncorks a beauty, a dream pitch, and the batter will get lucky and connect. Sometimes you'll throw a "waste" pitch—getting a batter to go after a bad one because you're ahead of him and can afford a ball if he doesn't swing—but the guy will luck out and hit the thing out of the park. I guess it averages out, though. Sometimes you'll make a mistake and serve it belt-high on a platter and he'll swing and miss. Man, I wish *that* would happen more often.

I was glad to see '59 end. New decades always thrill me.

7

Hurricane Donna, I Hate You

In '60, I had a Buffalo contract again, and after the same old haggling the Phillies and I settled on $700. I had down pat the science of sending contracts back. I'd always ask for more than I wanted and the Phils would up their offer a bit, and on the third go-round we agreed on a price. They usually paid me in thirty pieces of silver.

Having the Buffalo contract again encouraged me, and the raise further led me to believe that the Phils were still high on Jerry Kettle. Even if the idiot *did* ask for $900 that year!

I didn't get to rookie school in '60, because I'd had some Army problems in late '59. Babe Herman had contacted the National Guard and fixed me up with a special duty schedule, beating the Army out of my warm body. I

went on a six-month training tour of duty in November
'59, and didn't get discharged until the Phillies' spring
training was over.

While I was protecting everyone from the Bomb,
the Phils had optioned me out to the Indianapolis Indians, and that's where I found myself assigned when I
got out of Guard duty. The way I got sprung was un-
usual, too. It seems a big league club has a lot of influence
with the government, and vice versa. When I found out I
wouldn't be released until well after spring training, I
started writing letters all over the place looking for someone to turn the screws and get me out.

One fellow in my Guard unit, Bill Thom, played ball
at USC and was with the Boston organization. Thom
knew a congressman from the Los Angeles area and got
him to send a telegram. It must have shaken up the Fort,
I guess, because the next day the five of us who were pro
ballplayers were released and I was on my way to Indianapolis.

This is a fringe benefit, I suppose. A ballplayer who is
back east, say, and is supposed to attend National Guard
meetings on the West Coast, can explain his position and
between him and the ball club it's arranged for him to be
placed in a Control Group. This is a special group comprised of guys with special reasons why the attending of
meetings is infeasible. The Control Group then trains at
special times, rather than the normal two-week summer
encampment period the average guy attends. It's a good
deal, really, and, as you've gathered by this sterling prose,
all very special. The fringe benefit comes in when you

discover that nobody really notices the Control Group boys and the two-week period isn't as traumatic as the summer one. Like no KP, for instance, because since nobody cares about us, nobody knows we're around. It's kind of like spring training.

Indianapolis was Triple-A ball, and I knew it was probably my last crack at it. Freddie Hutchins, the former pitcher, was our manager.

I'll never figure out how the hell the Phillies' organization made its decisions in those days. They knew damn well I'd been in the service and that I hadn't been to spring training to get in shape. So what happens? I get Triple-A ball again and naturally fall on my face. I wasn't there two weeks before they had already used me for about six innings, to relieve in lost ball games. Needless to say, I got bombed every time out. I pitched three innings against Houston, when Ron Santo was playing there and Enos Slaughter was managing. Ron and some others rapped me good. I also pitched three innings against Minneapolis-St. Paul and they also knocked me out in short order. It was Mattoon all over again.

All the while I was trying like hell to catch up with the other guys, as far as condition went. Not having been to spring training, or playing any kind of regular competitive ball in the off season as I usually did, put me at a disadvantage. Then they put me in to pitch, I get bombed, and the disadvantage suddenly looks a hundred miles wide and the Philly bigwigs decide I'm no good.

Then they sent me to Asheville, North Carolina, in the Sally League, to get into better shape and sweat out the kinks. Hot weather always helps a guy work into form. In my case all it did was clean out my pores.

What happens? They pitch me right away again. I still wasn't ready but they pitched me anyway and before I knew it I was 1–3 or 2–4, I forget which.

There was a funny situation there at Asheville. They'd been having a bit of trouble winning ball games, it seems, and were starting out in the cellar again. It was one of those community-owned ball clubs, where a committee ran the team. If a manager didn't bring in a pennant, the town had a meeting to determine whether he stayed—and other top-drawer decisions. Bear in mind that these decisions are being made by people who wouldn't know a baseball from a casaba melon.

Consequently, the ball club looked like a *Who's Who?* Teams were sending top ballplayers to Asheville to help win a pennant and keep the committee happy. Or whoever the hell happened to be running the club that week. Ballplayers were coming in and out at the rate of two or three a day. Most of them were shaking their heads.

Charlie Crescent, the Asheville manager, will never win any brains contests. He took me aside one day and told me I was getting shipped out because they were juggling the team again in another effort to win some ball games and keep the town happy. I asked him where I was going, and Charlie the Diplomat said something like, "Dunno, kid. They'll probably release you."

Nothing like a little encouragement for the kids, eh?

General managers of ball clubs do a lot of long-distance calling and business chatting. They usually know which

clubs have what openings, and as a rule have their finger on the employment pulse around the leagues. I
started calling around and writing some letters, because
it's a good bet that if one club releases a guy, he'll at least
get a few tryouts with other organizations before he gets
presented with his hara-kiri knife. Somebody always
needs a pitcher, as one friend of mine put it.

I got word that my old friend Frank Lucchesi was managing the Williamsport Grays again and that was all I
needed. I packed my stuff and was there in two days.

Old Home Week once more. Harris was there, and
Figard and the rest, and Lucchesi had a big welcome
for me. He took me on the club and all of a sudden I was
playing A ball again for Williamsport. You *can* go home
again.

When I joined the Grays they were 3½ games out of
first place, battling like hell for the pennant with the
Springfield Giants, who had guys like Carl Boles, who's
now in the Biggies somewhere, and Charlie Dees, the first
baseman for the Angels, and Jim Duffalo, now with the
Giants and who ended up with a 13–5 season with Springfield in '60. The Giants had a good team.

I lost the first game I pitched, but then won the next
six straight. I could do no wrong, and I was being rotated every four days and winning like mad. Against good
competition, too. I felt like the guy whose suspected
tumor turned out to be an ingrown hair.

I went a nine-inning game against Reading, during this
stretch, which turned into a great game. I only gave them

six hits and didn't let a man get to third base. My clutch pitching was at its highest peak. Reading took two hits in each of the first, second and fifth, but when I bore down the pitches were going right where I wanted them to. Struck out seven and walked only two. The season was early, but we were already known as the Go-Go-Grays.

Then I pitched a good one against the Binghamton Triplets, too. We won it 3–2 in a real thriller, but I pitched steady, controlled ball. Despite giving them ten hits, I spaced them out so they didn't hurt. In that game, Tom Tresh hit me three-for-five, and Joe Pepitone got two off me. They've since gone on to greater things.

But for some reason, I was going good and going steadily. I think it may have been sheer fright. Charlie Crescent's words were still hurting.

I got some sweet revenge on Crescent, though. While he was down in Asheville sweating out finishing in last place again and getting the city council on his back, I was going great guns with Williamsport. I cut out all my clippings and sent them down to my old buddy Mack Burke, who was now catching for Asheville. Mack would wait until Crescent came into the clubhouse and then he'd shout, "Hey you guys, I got a letter from Kettle and he's just won his sixth straight game!" According to Mack's letters, Crescent was really burned up. I think that was the last year Crescent managed, too. Maybe Mack drove him nuts.

If that's the case and you're reading this, Mack, get in touch with me and I'll send you a check for a case of beer.

One day I was pitching against Binghamton and didn't

know that John Quinn, the Phillies' general manager, had flown over to look at me. I had a no-hitter for six innings, but a base hit and a walk started me out wrong in the seventh. They laid down a bunt to move the runners along, and Yours Truly picked it up and threw it into left field trying to force the guy at third. I'm also available for maiden voyage dedications.

I pitched a good game aside from that throwing error, though, and we won it 3–2. But I never did hear anything come of Quinn's scouting trip and I'm just wondering whether he was only looking for a good-fielding pitcher that day. Other than that, how'd you like the game, John?

I ended the season 11–3, having started 15 games and completed 9, compiling a 2.29 ERA. Helluva year, despite that wild throw in the Binghamton game and Tommy Tresh's disrespect.

Midway through the season we pulled way ahead of the second-place team and so, naturally, this was the point at which we went nuts off the field. We were winning and that's all that mattered. We felt like we could win whenever we chose, which wasn't too far from the truth.

Some things we did were just plain silly, like the time we were coming back from Albany and bought a crate of Bing cherries to eat on the trip. Bushels of cherries, and each guy had his own bagful. A few guys actually ate a few.

We found out early in the trip that if you hit the bus windows real hard, they swung outward on hinges and exposed you to a fabulous opening. Three guesses what happens when a winning ball team is given a crate of cherries, a bus with open windows and a long trip home.

Yeah, that's what we did. Didn't miss a car the whole trip. Had perfect control. For a change.

One time at Nashville I thought we'd really had it from goofing around. Lucchesi was sick that night and stayed in his room. We were staying on the seventh floor, and Lee Elia and Al Niger decided to throw a pitcher of water on a guy walking on the street below.

Some guy in a barbershop across the street said he saw which window it came out of, and when the hotel officials checked it out it happened to be my and Bob Milo's room. This old guy in a half-soaked suit, aided by the hotel manager, dragged us out and we all woke up Lucchesi. Frank was feeling particularly lousy and threatened to fine us, etc. The old guy left, muttering to himself about crazy athletes and silly baseball games. Lucchesi wanted to fine Milo and me $50, but we told him we hadn't done it. He asked if we knew who it was, we said no, and the whole thing was dropped. Frank was pretty mad, though, and if he wasn't so sick I'm sure *somebody* would have had a dented wallet.

One night we were in Springfield, and Gordy Figard and Lee Elia were standing Marco Mainini and Dick Harris in a shuffleboard game at one of the local pubs. If you've ever been to Springfield, you know that shuffleboard rates second in excitement to going down to the barbershop and watching a few haircuts.

Anyway, this was some sort of championship match, because all season these four had been playing shuffle-board with each other whenever we hit Springfield. Gordy and Lee finally won it, after heated competition and half a gross of beers, so Gordy picked Lee up on his shoulders and began running all over the place shouting about Victory. In one spot, he ran Lee's head smack through a masonite part of the ceiling.

We all laughed at the time, because here was Figard standing there with Elia on his shoulders, except you couldn't see Elia's head. When it was all over, Lee had a helluva bump, but Figard had twisted his neck and couldn't play the next night. We lost the game, incidentally, by one run, which made Gordy feel bad, but we reassured him by posting a notice on the front of the bus proclaiming Gordy's and Lee's prowess at shuffleboard. Gordy told Lucchesi he had fallen out of bed. On Elia, I guess.

We had a guy named Ted Sloan playing with us who was actually a bullpen catcher, because he wasn't getting much chance to play. His main duty was warming up the pitcher whenever Harris had made the last out and was putting on his gear in the dugout. Only Ted never came in from the bullpen in the ordinary jogging fashion.

Ted would get down on all fours, like a sprinter, and when someone yelled "Bang!" he'd run full speed into home plate. I mean, he'd really cut out and the fans would yell "Go, go, go!" all the way in. When he got to home there'd be more applause for him than the rest of us would hear all through the game.

One night we were expecting to play, but it was one of those nights when you didn't know whether it was going to quit raining or go on all night. It would pour for a few minutes, and then clear up so the groundkeepers could go out and straighten up the infield. Then it would sprinkle again, then clear up a minute or so later. It went on like this from six o'clock, which was when we showed up, to about eight or so. The umpires were just waiting around to see if it would stop long enough to at least start the game.

Finally it looked as if we were going to play, but by this time the field was soaked and we were hoping the game would be called anyway. Everyone thought the umps *would* call it, but there were still about 800 fans in the stands and the umps were huddling with the managers at home plate.

We were all in the dugout and suddenly we heard a *clop-clop-clop* from behind us. Sloanie was walking through the dugout and onto the field in a pair of swim fins and a diver's mask, complete with snorkel. He walked right onto the infield, with all this paraphernalia and his glove, pounding it and spitting in it like he was ready to play.

When the umps saw this they turned blue. They ranted and raved at Lucchesi, who was breaking up a bit himself, and finally Frank came over and ranted at Sloanie, telling him to get-that-stuff-the-hell-off-and-you're-fined-ten-bucks. Sloanie just turned slowly around and clopped back to the dugout, all the while pounding his glove and looking for all the world like the most disappointed base-ball player in history.

When he got to a particularly big puddle right near the first base line, he splashed his way through it and the fans went wild. I think everyone enjoyed the show but the umps. Lucchesi laughed, but only when he got back to the dugout.

Elia, our shortstop from Philadelphia, was hitting the ball real good one day during a home game, but he still couldn't buy a hit. His first smash went long and deep, but the right fielder made a circus catch of it. Lee's second time up he drove a sinking liner to center and the center fielder made a shoestring catch.

His third and probably last time up, he belted a high line drive toward left field, a sure hit for him, but the shortstop got the Spirit in him or something and leaped up to make a fantastic one-handed catch of it. Lee was so mad and frustrated he turned around first and ran full blast to the dugout, sliding in headfirst and scraping his arms. He was going faster than he thought, and came steaming right into the bench. Gordy Figard jumped out with his hat on backwards and gave an overly demonstrative "Safe" sign, yelling the word at the top of his lungs. The crowd roared.

In the clubhouse after the game, Lucchesi announced to us that Gene Martin, the Philly farm director, was sitting in the stands that day, right behind the dugout. He fined Lee $10, suspended him, and told Gordy that Jocko Conlon wanted to talk to him. Nobody thought it was very funny, especially Pete Cera, who used up two bottles of Merthiolate on Lee's arms.

I've never received a serious injury on the field, but I came pretty close to one that season. I was pitching and had a man on first, one time, and when I delivered the next pitch I heard "There he goes!" behind me. I turned around as fast as I could to watch Harris' peg and the play at second, going into a crouch as I did so. I could hear the whooshing of the ball, but when it hit me in the small of the back, you could have knocked me over with a feather —as the saying goes. I sprawled out flat, the breath knocked out of me.

When I rolled over and looked back, Lucchesi was screaming out across the infield to see if I was hurt, but I could see Harris' nice white teeth showing through his mask. He was laughing like hell.

So that's the way '60 went. That's the way it *always* went when you were winning, but had I known that '60 would go down in history as my last good year—my last chance to make it—I would have whooped it up even more. I had matured enough and calmed down enough to have the Biggies cinched. Our team was so good we ran ahead of the pack for most of the season and clinched the pennant with about two weeks to go—something like 15 games ahead. This type of competitive assurance always helps the individual ballplayers, but sometimes it also gives them a false sense of security and might even knock a few games off your win-loss record or give your ERA a kick in the pants. As I say, if I'd known '60 was the beginning of the end . . .

The team did slack off a bit. Lucchesi was getting worried when we lost something like our last ten games that year, because the top four teams were slated for playoffs and Frank was wondering whether we were getting a little bit too complacent. We weren't even going out for batting practice, we were so cocky. We'd tinker around the clubhouse a bit and only when the umpires came out for the game's start would we come out on the field. It must have looked like we were really a vaudeville act—no batting practice, no fielding practice, and then trudge out on the field and lose. Yeah, I'm sure Lucchesi thought it was mass hypnosis or something.

I pitched the first playoff game, against Reading, and Rod Taylor (now with the Cards) and I really battled it out. The game too might have been my best of the year.

It was 0–0 going into the bottom of the ninth. In fact, Rod and I each had a no-hitter until the fourth, and it was I who got the first hit off him—and he who got the first hit off me! When you talk about pitchers' duels, you *gotta* admit the phrase was coined for games like this.

I led off the bottom of the ninth, and Rod walked me. I remember smirking out at him as I trotted down the line. I'm sure Rod will remember that walk even years from now. I know I will.

Alex Cosmidis, our veteran, bunted me over to second, and then Ted Savage rammed his first pitch to the opposite field and I came across with the winning and only run.

I think I stomped so hard on home plate it may have registered five or six on Cal Tech's earthquake scales way out in Pasadena.

The game was called "one of the finest pitching duels ever witnessed at Bowman Field" by the Williamsport *Sun-Gazette,* and I'd be the first to agree. We had only three hits for the whole game, mine and Savage's two, all singles. Reading had five. For six straight innings, Reading got their leadoff man on base, but I was beautiful in the clutch. I walked four, Taylor only walked one. Up until the ninth we had only two baserunners, Savage and me with our singles. Savage managed to get to third in his inning, but otherwise nobody got to second for us. Taylor had retired the first eight guys to face him, and after my single he got the next ten out before Savage's first hit. In the last five innings, Reading left eight men on base.

It was one helluva game. It only lasted one hour and 59 minutes and I needed only 98 pitches, counting two intentional walks. The only thing that marred that gorgeous day was two errors committed by our side.

Interesting sidelight: Savage is now with the Pirates, Taylor's with the Cards. The third hero, me, is now a has-been ballplayer doing landscaping in Pasadena. Fortune, thy name is rhododendrons.

As long as Ted Savage, a Negro, was the hero of that game, this seems a good time for a few comments on Negro ballplayers in the minors. In most places the Negro ballplayer has no particular problems, but in the South he has a rough go of it. Often he has to be housed in different areas than his white teammates, and he must eat in different places. Some leagues, in fact, prohibit Negro ballplayers altogether.

The Sally League was never too bad, but in '57 in the Carolina League I got the impression nobody in the stands knew or cared a goddam thing about baseball—they just came out to the game to torment the colored players. Greensboro was especially bad.

We had a third baseman named John Kennedy, who had already been up with the Phils but who had been sent down to us this year. Poor John, who was a damn good ballplayer, really got it. Favorite remarks by the local gentry: "Look at that monkey swinging at third base!" "Hey, burrhead [or steel wool-head or apeman], whoever told you you could put that white uniform on?" There are other similar bits of intelligence, but I won't cite them. Some idiot might read it and become delirious because he got quoted. Burrhead was a favorite name for the colored boys, though.

It's interesting seeing a crowd riding a colored ballplayer and then the guy wins the game for the home team. When this happens there are a few polite claps, maybe, if you can call a Southern bigot polite, but it's generally forgotten by the time he crosses home plate. The difference is very noticeable between that instance and when a *white* player wins the game. Pitifully noticeable.

Making an error opens all the flood gates. Where a white player will get a few boos and the standard derisions, the colored player making an error becomes "nigger," "black man," "black burrhead," etc. It hurts to see it, but I'm sure some of the colored players will agree with me that it certainly hurts a lot more to see these animals fill the stands and realize that you're *their* home team. Like finding out Adolf Eichmann was your uncle.

In Hipoint we had three local guys playing with us: Jack Taylor, a pitcher, Freddie Harrington, a shortstop, and Billy Ford, a second baseman. All three were native Hipointers and lived there year-round. The interesting thing is that these guys would come up to the colored guys after a game, say when the latter were down in the dumps after a rough afternoon, and try to tell them not to worry about all the cruel remarks and cursing. We'd stand around shaking our heads wondering what we could tell the colored guys to cheer them up, but this trio had a good solution. "What the hell," they'd tell our colored teammates, "you guys have it made. Look at us; we have to stay here all year *long* with these clods!"

It always seems to take something away from the game when one segment of the fans is roped off from the others and one segment of your team is treated like lepers. Baseball is a beautiful sport. It's too bad some of the fans that follow it have to be mental lepers themselves.

Picture this: In spring training with Buffalo one year, all the colored players approached the club and threatened to go home because they weren't being treated equally *by the club*. They were living in a colored section, rooming with colored folks who were paid to feed them. The only trouble was, the club was giving the people some ridiculous price to feed the players—something like

$2.50 for three meals a day—when we were getting $5 a day for food, and check-signing privileges at the hotel. The Phillies were paying the boarding families about half as much to feed our colored teammates!

So the guys raised hell, justifiably, and the Phillies finally decided they were human beings after all like the rest of us and gave the families a sensible amount of money for food.

Negroes didn't have the freedom we had. We went to dog races, jai alai games and shows, but they weren't admitted. Because of this, we never could really *feel* like teammates. The Negroes would come in, suit up and play, and then go right home after the game. When asked "How's it going, buddy?" or some such, they'd reply "Fine" and that would be it. They kept pretty much to themselves and I suppose you can't blame them. No man is completely insensitive to mass abuse.

There isn't much you can tell young colored kids just starting out. Prejudice is all around us whether we like it or not, so the only thing you can say to them is just to hang in there and remember that they won't be in the South all their lives—hopefully. Hell, even when the Giants brought up Willie McCovey he couldn't stay downtown in San Francisco. Not having a home yet, he had to stay at the Booker T. Washington Hotel, not one of the better places downtown.

The only thing you can tell them is just to stick it out. Things *have* to get better.

Anyway, Ted Savage came through that day and we

went wild after the game. Gordy Figard met me at the plate and I carried him and Ted on my back all the way to the dugout. Lucchesi was delirious. Here was his overly complacent team, coming through in the clutch and out-classing the competition. We won when we had to; other-wise, the hell with it. Right, Frank?

But as happy as we were that day for coming through in the first game of the playoffs for the Governor's Cup, it was nothing like the night we mathematically clinched the pennant, about 10 days before. Lucchesi, after that game, had fifteen cases of beer and a couple of cases of cham-pagne waiting in the clubhouse. This for only 22 players, yet!

Man, did we drink! Everyone was wild. Sportswriters came in and we'd dump champagne all over them. Even the opposing team's manager stopped by and had a few beers with us. I was drenched from head to toe with booze, and Lucchesi looked like he'd taken a bath in the stuff.

The wives of the married players would always wait about twenty feet down the hall outside our dressing room for their husbands to come out. There were about eight or nine of them outside this evening, and I decided to shoo them off so we could continue our celebration into the night. This was after about forty-five minutes of champagne and beer—I was really flying. I was dressed in socks, shorts and my uniform shirt, but I didn't care be-cause I was on top of the world and by now pretty certain I had a good future.

Confronted with this specter, this drunk and soaked

seminaked baseball pitcher, the women screamed to high heaven. I told them they'd have to go home, as their loved ones were celebrating each other and would continue to do so for at least five more hours. Between blushes and giggles, they grudgingly left and went back to their knitting, or whatever wives do when their husbands just won a pennant and are getting smashed in the clubhouse.

I guess I must have made an ass of myself in those last games of that season. I was feeling great, my arm was healed, and I was chomping at the bit to pitch more games. The best part of the whole year was that Lucchesi would only pitch me against the top teams, the teams that were threatening to close the gap on us. So while my 10–3 record in the regular season was good, I knew and the Phillies knew that it was compiled against top contenders, the best teams in the league. And I owe a lot for the good season, after my poor start and sore arm, to a guy named Norm Camp, who was our pitching coach on the Grays that year.

Norm wouldn't bother the guys the night before they were scheduled to pitch, or the morning after they did pitch, but in between he'd work us like dogs. He ran us hard and ran us ragged. It paid off. In that 1–0 game with Reading, I felt as if I could have gone nine more innings, I was in such good shape. I whooped it up at every opportunity, believe me, but I'll always give Norm Camp his due for keeping me in such good shape. In fact, it's a tribute to Norm to look over the top ten pitchers in the Eastern League that season. We had four of them.

We beat Reading again, and then when Springfield came in for the rest of the playoffs, Norm pitched and shut them out right off. He pitched a great game, beating Corky Johnson, who had won 15 in the regular season.

The Reading series was two-out-of-three, which we won, but the Springfield series was to be three-out-of-five, for the Shaugnessey Cup. Norm beat them that first game and I was scheduled to go in the second.

It's some kind of comment on how my career was shaping up that Hurricane Donna blew in that day and it rained for seven days. In the minors they can't afford to carry salaries too long, so the series was canceled completely. My bit was chomped clear through.

Packing for home, I made it a point to buy about a dozen copies of the *Sun-Gazette,* and I mailed the following column ahead of me. That's how good I felt and how confident I was that the next season would be the one to shoot me straight up to the Biggies.

It's by Mike Bernardi, associate sports editor, from his "Sports Mike" column:

KETTLE SETTLES SCORE

The big guy had a score to settle.

Six-foot, five-inch Jerry Kettle, the righthander from Pasadena, Calif., waited exactly one year to settle it.

A year ago, after a not too successful season, Kettle was given the assignment by Williamsport Manager Frank Lucchesi of trying to pitch the Grays "technically" into the second place in the Eastern League standings.

The Grays and Allentown finished in a dead heat for the runner-up position behind champion Springfield and on orders from Eastern League President Thomas H. Richardson a sudden-death playoff was set up.

Kettle, pitching against Allentown's Bill Thom, was beaten 6–1. He was tagged for home runs by Dick McCarthy and Jerry Mallett as the A-Sox earned the right to host the first two games in the best of three semifinal series for the Governors' cup.

It was Kettle's 10th loss against nine wins and there were those who said the big guy would never make it. He didn't have the desire.

That was a year ago and minus a six months' tour of service with Uncle Sam.

ACE OF STAFF, "DARLING" OF FANS

Since joining the Grays from Asheville of the Sally League, Kettle, affectionately called the "Hubber" by his teammates, has become not only the ace of the Williamsport pitching staff but a "darling" of the fans.

Last night, after a 10–3 regular season, the native Californian was given the task of getting the champion Grays off on the right foot in the playoffs after a poor finish which saw them lose nine out of their last 10 games.

And what a job the "Hubber" turned in. He blanked Reading, 1–0, on five singles to give the Grays that all-important first-game win in a short series. Not only did he pitch shutout ball but he got the first of three Williamsport hits and scored the game's only run in the ninth after working Ron Taylor for a walk. He rode home from second on a single by Ted Savage and jumped into the waiting arms of Gordy Figard, who greeted him at home plate.

The 22-year-old, who has the scouts talking this season, needed only 98 pitches to win one of the biggest games of his career. Over the first four innings when he pitched hitless ball, he threw only 40 pitches. His toughest inning was the seventh when he needed 16 to retire the Indians.

98 Pitches Include Intentional Walks

The 98 pitches become an even more remarkable feat when it's pointed out that Kettle issued two intentional walks—both to Mike White—to get to Taylor.

The route-going performance by Kettle, which also blanked Reading on July 16, was exactly the tonic the tired Grays' pitching staff needed.

Prior to the game, in his dressing room cubicle, Lucchesi said, "What we need is to have Jerry go all the way. He'll be in there as long as he can and if I have to go to the bullpen the only one there will be Baldwin [Dave].

"We really were hurting with all those double-headers [three in four days] and our pitching staff not up to par. If Kettle can go all the way tonight, then we'll be back in order.

"It'll be Siebler [Dwight] Wednesday night and then it depends upon how Camp [Norm] feels. He tried his arm out tonight in the batting practice and reported no soreness. He could be ready to go in a couple days."

Camp, a 12-game winner and a real veteran, suffered an injury to his pitching shoulder Aug. 31 against Reading. He was forced to retire from the game after pitching two hitless innings.

Most Tense, Best Pitched of Season

After the game Lucchesi, the master strategist who twice foiled Reading's bid to break the scoreless duel by going to the intentional walk, called the battle "the most tense and best pitched of the season."

"There have been other thrillers during the year where we were forced to come from behind. But this one had everything riding on every pitch. You just couldn't afford to make a mistake."

It was pointed out that Taylor's walk to Kettle was the only one he issued in his last two outings against the Grays. Williamsport made the most of his "Mistake" by turning it into the game-winning run.

The only disappointment last night was the crowd. Only 710 came out to see Williamsport's first championship team in 26 years start its quest for an Eastern League "double." All that can be said is that thousands missed one of the finest ball games ever played at Bowman Field.

How about *that* jazz?

8

A Phil and His Money
Are Soon Parted

*W*hen the Greatest Pitcher in Baseball got his contract in January of '61, he honestly thought he'd be getting a shot with the Phillies. After that great year in '60, after I'd recovered from a sore arm and even got into great shape after being shuffled around like an old fungo bat (thanks again, Norm!), and after my greatest string of wins and important clutch ball games, I honestly thought I'd get the rookie school bit, be invited to stay over for spring training with the Phillies and then go on up with Dallas Green, Art Mahaffey and the rest.

The decision to send a kid up from the minors to the Biggies is largely one of records. The organization goes a lot by the kid's overall records and the manager's weekly reports on how the kid is doing, his attitudes, his problems, his strong points. A manager, through his reports and his own design, can make or break a kid on the way up. I don't believe it ever happens, but if a manager has the gout or a pretty good carbuncle, this alone *could* determine whether a kid ever makes it. A phone call from the parent club, asking whether a kid is ready, a manager feeling rotten or a little P.O.'d at the kid momentarily—this could wreck the kid's chances.

Conversely, if the manager's in a good mood and is high on the kid on that certain day, the kid could get sent up without really being ready. Managers have a heavy responsibility, don't let anyone kid you.

Personally, I have no gripes about most of the guys I played with. Lucchesi was far and above the best manager I ever played for. It would do some club a lot of good to consider him seriously for a Biggie manager's spot some day. For example, Lucchesi was with Salt Lake City in C ball when I first met him, and when I bowed out he was managing Chattanooga, a Double-A club. Right now he's managing Little Rock, a Triple-A club. I know he's going to make it. He's a great manager for a contending club, a little on the order of the Leo Durocher type.

Another consideration the club makes when evaluating a kid is how much dough is invested in him. If he's a big bonus baby, say, even with a mediocre year the chances are good he'll get a crack at the Biggies. The club simply wants to get its money back and often figures there's nothing else to lose by sending him up. If he pans out, it was a good investment. If not, they'll write it off and the kid's had it because the club won't waste much time on him anymore. If the kid signed cheap, or otherwise doesn't represent much dough to the club, he's liable to spend a lot of time in the bushes—the minors.

The reason they call the minors the bushes is simple: the minors are full of hard-working insects. This is a bit of a paradox, which I think I've hinted at before. A club will give a guy a large bonus, strictly on speculation, and bring the kid up for the big test. But sometimes the kid they're really high on, a no-bonus struggler, will never get a crack at it. Baseball is a money game, and it's a damn big business. Ball club owners aren't in it for the sport, believe me. Walter O'Malley didn't go to Los Angeles because he was nuts about palm trees.

Dave Nicholson, now with Baltimore, was a hundred-grand bonus baby, but had a terrible year at Little Rock in '61. Next year he was up with Baltimore in the Biggies and now he's going pretty good. Bo Belinsky only had fair years in the minors, and he got a crack at it.

Being an ex-minor leaguer, I only get a little peeved when I read about some extra large bonus being handed to a kid. I got peanuts. But there's one thing you don't knock, and that's making a major league ball club. You feel more power to 'em, and that's that. It's like knocking the President because you don't think he qualifies.

He's there and you're here. So take off, buddy.

Anyway, the contract I got in '61 was the same old rag calling for Buffalo, with a lousy $100 raise. The first thought that came to my mind, after I'd calmed down and my mom and dad had taken off the straightjacket, was that every time I'd gone through this Buffalo crap with Kerby Farrell, I'd been short-changed on the deal. I'd be damned if I'd go through it again, and by God I was going to get a large economy-sized raise after that great '60 season. Of course, the Phillies didn't agree with me.

I want to get something straight before I sound off again and get sued for something. I like the Phillies. They are a great ball club and a contender, after that great season last year. They have some great players and an excellent, really fine pitching staff. And it bugs me that I'm not up there with them. But unless they've made some changes I'm not aware of, which is quite probable, mind you, the Phillies have a very poor front office organization.

Now don't tell me how they've built up a pennant contender. They "Whiz Kidded" themselves to a pennant in '50, and it's been 14 years since anyone even *thought* of the Phillies as still being in the National League. Don't tell me how they've built up . . . I said that, didn't I?

So.

So the contract trouble began again, this time in dead earnest. I sent the thing back and went to spring training with Buffalo. What the hell—I wanted to play ball, didn't I?

I should mention here that in the winter of '60 I did my little bit to help the Phillies edge me out. I was working out at Jefferson School in Pasadena, and got into a football game. Tackle, yet, but no protective equipment. It was a pretty stupid thing to do, but Superman threw a block at one guy who was running for the money, and came up with a shoulder separation—my pitching shoulder. At first I didn't notice too much discomfort, but then my shoulder started paining. The pain eventually got so bad I went to a doctor—*two weeks later*—and he treated me for it.

I was due to leave March 10 for spring training, so I didn't say anything to the Phillies, fearing it would ruin my career. The arm was still in a sling in February, but at the time I reported, nobody knew I'd been hurt at all.

I think that injury, combined with the shoddy maneuvering of the players by the Phillies before eventually sending me to Chattanooga in '61, was my professional downfall. 1961 was the top of the ninth for Jerry Kettle.

If there's one thing I hope some kid who wants to play ball learns from this book—if his parents let him read it—it's *always speak up when you're hurting.* The club will do everything to help you out of it and they have the equipment and the specialists to do it. You'll never get anywhere playing with a sore arm or a Charley horse or whatever, and you'll probably wind up doing yourself more harm than good.

So I didn't say anything about being hurt and my arm having been inactive for quite a spell when I reported to Buffalo.

1961 was the season about five or six guys refused to sign, but still went to spring training. In all fairness, I guess '61 might have been the year the Phillies got sick of the cellar and decided to let Ford Frick know they were still around. But there were several guys who were ready to throw in the towel because of the razamatazz we got, financial and otherwise.

The Phillies wrecked my career this year only because of stupid, moronic executive decisions that were made about who should play where and why.

(By the way, why do they always call the guys who don't sign "hold outs?" Why isn't the parent club called a holdout? Is it *really* true, since baseball is the most prevalent form of slavery in the country, that the *player* is always wrong?)

So anyway, I worked out without getting too bugged by the Phils, but there were three guys who bought fishing gear and went out every day for a long while and fished their heads off, refusing even to work out. I won't mention their names, but they were right and the Phils were wrong. It was one of the first clues, which I didn't pick up at the time, to what kind of a year it was going to be. Career-wise, I mean. I got a championship ring in '61 because I played on a great team, not because *I* did anything great, but it was essentially over that spring. Something was going on in the Phils' front office. Something like blindman's bluff with real-life pitchers.

The Phils finally got all of them signed, but with me they kept going round and round. Jim Newton was the paper man again this year, the general manager. I suppose I might have been a litttle presumptuous reminding Jim that the Williamsport Grays were three games behind when I joined the club in '60, and even after I hadn't been allowed to get into decent shape we went on to bag the pennant with 15 games to spare, as well as winning that playoff with Reading.

With that as my main argument, Newton came back true to form and told me how the Phils were actually very disappointed in me. His reasoning was that I'd been given three chances at Triple-A ball and still hadn't made it. I guess he was forgetting about the time I had a Triple-A club made but was shipped out because the Phillies decided Don Cardwell would keep the city council happy; or the time Indianapolis expected me to go nine innings right off the bat after National Guard service.

In short, he made me feel like hell, even though I wasn't agreeing with a single word he said. General managers must attend a club-paid psychology course every season. Some day a man will get elected President of the United States not because he's a politician but because he was a minor league general manager. He'll be the kind of guy who'd tell Julius Caesar he was sorry for not having stabbed in the proper place. And get away with it.

So Newton came up with a brilliant move. He told me they'd put a clause in my contract giving me $750, and if I made the Buffalo club for 24 days, until the first cutdown, they'd up me to $900. I was kind of sick arguing with them and was still at a confidence peak and sure I'd make Buffalo, so I signed.

Listen to this. It's impossible, like Hurricane Donna. The Phillies, *the day before the Buffalo opening day,* cut down Dwight Siebler and sent him to Buffalo. I had the ball club made, but guess who got sent out? I had made it! I was told by the manager I had made it! Nobody, no place, can ever convince me the Phillies weren't saving $150 a month by cutting Kettle off the Buffalo roster. Hell, they could have sent Siebler to Miami, another Triple-A club, right?

Right. *Damn* right.

So out I went, and all of a sudden was playing ball for peanuts again. But listen, the plot thickens.

So I packed up and was sent to the Double-A and A camp, the teams being Chattanooga and Williamsport, respectively. I was pretty P.O.'d, disappointed and just plain mad. My confidence, that great booster and helper of kids on the way up, was smashed to smithereens. I was starting to think I needed to pitch a 20–0 season with an ERA of 0.00 to get a crack even at this cellar-place club. You'd think they were worried that my coming up for a crack at the Phillies would lose them a pennant! I don't even think any of them could *spell* "pennant."

Now the most rotten thing of all happened. Chattanooga, the Double-A team, had broken camp the same day I was cut from Buffalo, and when I got to Plant City, they were gone. I knew by this time that I'd be playing for Chattanooga, because Lucchesi was now the manager there and I had earned *at least* a crack at Double-A ball. There are certain things you know, and there are certain things you assume. I *knew* I'd be playing at Chattanooga and the Phillies damn well knew it too.

But the Phils were consistent. They picked four guys—

Kinders, a catcher; Al Niger, and Bob Milo, two lefties; and me—and sent us to the A and B camp. We were all going to play for Chattanooga, but the Phils wanted to let Lucchesi play a few other guys for a few weeks, just so the Phils could say they gave them a chance. We should have gone right to Chattanooga, because they had started playing.

The Phillies didn't have the nerve to send us right there and make a cut at Chattanooga then, which is exactly the thing they did with me at Buffalo. There's a consistency in inconsistency, isn't there?

So we stayed in Plant City for two stinking weeks, not doing a goddam thing. We weren't even throwing. Andy Seminic, the ex-catcher, was managing Williamsport this year, and he was too busy trying to find out who would be playing on his team to bother with us. I don't blame him, of course, because he too knew we'd be going to Chattanooga so why should he bother with us when he had his hands full trying to form up his own team?

There we were being batting practice pitchers for an A club. We were pretty upset, because we were all ready to start playing for Chattanooga. Hell, I was even a first base *umpire* a few times! Milo was a mound ump once. Double-A ballplayers with a team already made, and we're umping for an A club—not throwing a stitch of baseball.

It was kind of funny, though. We were staying at the Hotel Plant City, which was the biggest place in town but a raunchy dump. Across the street from it they were tearing down an old building to make space for a new one, and every mosquito in the joint was moving across the street to the Plant City, our hotel. We spent most of our time scratching—literally. When you think about it, I guess the Plant City was such a dump even the mosquitoes preferred to stay in an abandoned joint across the street.

Bob Milo was a good pitcher who had been around for years and was just kind of treading water. The year before he'd won 18 games with a last-place club in Double-A ball, which is fairly hard to do. But Bob was also a great comedian. With us rotting in Plant City while the Chattanooga Lookouts were already playing ball, we were getting completely out of shape. We were all set to go when we got there, but who can stay in shape by umpiring inter-squad games? We were falling apart, so the next best thing to do, natch, was goof off. Milo and I led the parade.

Dennis Bennett and Ed Lunsford were in one room down the hall. Harry Oliver, a big pitcher, was in another room nearby. Milo and I were rooming together in a third room at the end of the hall. Milo had a magazine and we decided to use a photo of some girl to get Oliver out of his room to settle a phony argument about whether the gal was beautiful or not. While Oliver was across the hall settling the argument with Bennett and Lunsford, Milo and I went into his room and filled his bed with shaving cream.

We crept back down the hall to our room and waited for Oliver to come out. We saw him walking around in his skivvies, going back to bed. He was shaking his head over why in hell Bennett and Lunsford got into such a stupid argument in the first place. A minute or so later we saw his light go out. The place was deathly quiet.

"All right, you sons of bitches!" was the next thing we heard. Milo and I were laughing like hell, and we then saw Harry come raving out of his room like a lion with a hernia, shaking a can of shaving cream and all the while yelling, "I know why you got me out of my room, you bastards! Beautiful girl, my ass!"

Next thing—and Milo and I were folded up on the floor in tears laughing by this time—Oliver goes storming into Bennett's and Lunsford's room and the two of them are pleading with Oliver not to let them have it because they hadn't done a goddam thing.

Then Oliver goes storming back into his own room and Bennett and Lunsford are ranting to beat the band. We'd heard the shhhh-ing when Oliver let them have it point-blank. So then Bennett comes out with a big pail of water and into Oliver's room, and we hear a great *splash!* punctuated by Oliver screaming again about how he's going to castrate everyone in the goddam hotel. Milo and I were having a hard time breathing by this time. The hotel was so raunchy and dark that Milo and I were on our knees laughing, with our door half open so that nobody could see us.

In about ten minutes, there were eight or nine guys running from room to room, throwing water all over hell and making more noise than a hungry tiger in an echo chamber. Everyone but Milo and me, who had started the whole thing. We were buckled up with laughter, but by this time didn't have to stifle it.

Next thing, an old bellhop came up to our floor and started in with the "Awright, you guys, what's going on here" bit. He started walking down the hall to find out, and we could hear him squish along the soaked carpets. He started trying to chew out the guys about how wet the walls and carpets were, but he got blasted with a bucket of water from an anonymous doorway.

The poor guy ran down the hall, threatening to tell the manager and have us thrown out of the place. We, of course, were hoping somebody *would* throw us out and punish us by sending us to Chattanooga.

Ross Miller, who was assistant to our boss, Gene Martin, the farm director—his private secretary or something —came up in about ten minutes. Ross was kind of a finky guy anyway, but he really looked funny squishing down the hall in his bathrobe trying to be as stern as possible.

Ross said something like "Mr. Martin will hear about this," and one of us made an excellent suggestion as to what Ross could do with his bathrobe, Mr. Martin and the whole farm system. Then Ross suggested that we'd be sent home for wrecking the place, and we whooped and hollered like it was the greatest news since VJ-day.

By this time Milo and I had decided that discretion was the better part of valor, so we'd gotten into bed and were pretending we were asleep. The only trouble was, we could hear all this commotion through the transom and were still laughing like hell. We could hear Bennett, who by now was on to us, telling Ross Miller to check us out, but we'd barricaded our door with two chairs and a dresser.

Eventually, everyone just walked back into their rooms, and Ross was left standing in the middle of the hall talking to himself in his bathrobe. When he squished back down the hall, the place went wild laughing, which was a lot better than sleeping pills. He never did anything about it—no trouble or anything—but the next morning the carpet still squished when we went down to breakfast. Milo and I escaped unscathed.

So that's how you get to Chattanooga.

When we finally got there, I was out of shape again. In the first game I pitched, I had two out in the second inning and had just struck out the third guy except that Kinders let the ball get past him and roll to the backstop. After that I was shook up, I guess, and they rapped me good until I was yanked. (Don't forget, Kinders was one of the guys they were shuffling around with us before sending us there.) I started again in about five days, but I was still real wild and got knocked out in short order.

No excuses. I just wasn't in shape, that's all. I'd spent about 19 days getting out of shape because the Phillies were too chicken to cut a few kids from Chattanooga, and I just didn't have it when I finally got there.

In that whole year at Chattanooga, something like 150 ball games, I pitched a grand total of 44 innings. My record at the finish line was a whopping 1–4. No gripe about Lucchesi not playing me; he had a pennant to win and the Phillies' mistakes certainly weren't his concern.

One time when I was 0–3 and had been working real hard on the sidelines for a while with a catcher named

Dick Teed, who helped me a lot in trying to get into shape, I won a ball game 8–3. It was 8–0 going into the eighth, but they rapped me a few good ones to score three times. I had the game won easy, though, and felt I finally had it and could win a few ball games. But I didn't pitch again for ten days and was out of it once more by then, so I got bombed and earned my fourth loss. I never pitched again that season.

Just to show you how things go, we were a game and a half ahead of the Tiger club nearing the end of the season and within range of the pennant, but instead of going with the guys who were winning, like Milo or John Boozer, they decided on me. And I was a nothing then. They still had confidence in me, but why did they have to pick *then?*

By the third inning, I had struck out five of the first nine guys I faced, and we were ahead 1–0. It had been raining and the pressure was now on to win the game. But the rain got harder, and looked like it would keep up for days, so they called the game. I think I would have gone on to pitch a pretty good game, but those are the breaks.

Yes, the breaks. The weatherman and I have a personality clash.

We went on to win the pennant at Shreveport, and it was all over. My worst year, after a string of pretty good seasons, and it was only about 30 percent my own fault. If they'd sent us to Chattanooga when they were supposed to, when we were all in great shape, the year would have turned out much better. Like maybe I would have broken a leg, or something.

That winter was the longest yet. All I had to show for the previous season was a championship ring. Worth about $20.

Which is what anyone wouldn't have given for my chances next season.

In '62 I got my contract and was optioned out by the Phils to Dallas-Fort Worth. I already had two strikes against me—as we say in the trade—after that poor previous year, so I couldn't holler too much. Dallas-Fort Worth was an Angel organization. They took spring training about an hour's drive from my home in Pasadena—in Fullerton, California. The Phils were saving *more* money.

I knew everyone was going by last year's record, because in the entire Dallas-Fort Worth spring training I only pitched three innings. I also knew I'd had it.

They kept me there for the whole spring training season, and just before we were leaving they told me they were returning me to Philadelphia. The Phillies then gave me my release. It was the bottom of the ninth.

With two out, yet.

Hawaii, in the PCL, was training in San Bernardino, California, also fairly near my home, and Irv Noren was the manager. Irv's from Pasadena and I knew him pretty well, so I figured I'd give it a go—try out for Irv's team.

I phoned him to see if I could get a tryout before they were due to leave in a few days, and Irv told me to come down. He had a pitcher who was going home with a sore arm and Irv had been looking about for a replacement.

I went over and worked out with him and he told me he'd let me know before they pulled out for Hawaii. I went home to wait it out. He called one night and said they were leaving in the morning and did I still want to go over with them.

I did.

I was only in Hawaii three weeks. I pitched one inning. During that inning I hung a high slider—I'll never forget it—to a guy who belted a double and knocked in two runs. Hell, I figured two runs in one inning was pretty good for a guy who only pitched three innings all spring training.

The thing is, you have to be sharp. You have to be in shape, able to sweat easily, and be generally sharp. Which means you have to work in spring training. That's the whole idea of spring training. But I'd been shuffled around like a dead mouse by the Phillies and then Dallas-Fort Worth, so how could I get in shape and pitch? When I went to Hawaii, I expected to be worked in gradually and get into some semblance of shape. When I gave up that two runs in one inning, that was it.

So I learned how to make a Mai-Tai—big deal.

I know a player can get into shape himself, but it's pretty difficult. There is nothing like actual game conditions—inter-squad games, pitching to win something. It's like any other sport: if you're not mentally ready, there's no sense being physically ready. And the game-conditions part of spring training—the inter-squad games and exhibition games—is for that purpose: to get the guys in mental shape.

The trouble with the minor leagues is that the young kids have it tough to begin with, inasmuch as the teams there have only a manager by himself—sometimes a coach —who can't devote lots of time to pitchers, infielders, etc. In the Biggies, and in the higher minor leagues, they have coaches all over the place, one for pitchers to see that they get into shape, one for catchers, one for batting, etc. Therefore everyone gets worked and each has the same chance. In the minors, it's very seldom someone gets especially assigned to see that the pitchers get into shape.

After that Hawaii inning, I never pitched again. That year in Chattanooga did it, and the spring training in Fullerton was just a farce. Dallas-Fort Worth, in fact, kept all the young guys who weren't anything, and for some strange reason let all the guys with a winning season behind them go. Like Milo, who had a pretty decent year at Chattanooga. I know *I* had a bum year, but they must have known I had something after '58, '59 and '60. Yet they kept the young guys and let the old farts—I was twenty-three then—go back to the Phillies. The Phils let Milo go, too. And he played two seasons of Triple-A.

What a waste of time.

It was all over. Babe Herman, who was good friends with Roy Hamey and who had gone with the Yankees sometime during my minor league career, tried to pull me out of it.

Babe eventually left the Yanks, though, and when I had that great year in '59 with Williamsport, Babe was in a meeting with the Mets in New York and tried to get

Casey Stengel to draft me for $20,000. But the Mets didn't want to spend the money, which might be a philosophy indicating why they have succeeded the Phils as Cellar Lords. Nothing against Casey, but after looking at the Mets' record the past few years, who the hell would put money in Stengel's bank?

Anyway, when I got released by Hawaii, Babe got Johnny Pesky, who was managing Seattle, to come down and look at me and maybe give me a chance with his team. I felt I was through playing ball long before Babe thought so.

That's not quite right. Babe still doesn't think I'm through. Last winter Babe called and asked whether I'd be interested in trying out for some team or other. And just last month Babe called and wanted me to start throwing a bit to start getting back into shape.

God bless you, Babe. If you ever need some shrubbery, come around to Kettle's Nursery and I'll fix you up.

You get a dozen beers with every purchase.

9

⊖

Yeah, but Who the Hell Is Jerry Kettle?

*B*y now a hundred dozen people are probably wondering whether they can sue me, and an equal number are saying to themselves: "What's this crumb whining about? So he didn't make it—big deal!"

I don't know. I won't get sued, because those who would want to are the first ones who would realize the veracity of what I've said, and those who won't want to are probably rich already. As for the second part, well, I guess this crumb is whining about just that: I didn't make it and I wish to hell I was up there right now with Dallas Green and Art Mahaffey and Dennis Bennett and Bobby Wine and the rest of them. I'm sure Dick Harris and Gordy

Figard—two of my best friends now—would agree with this sentiment. We just signed the right contract at the wrong time, that's all.

It boils down to this: if you're a first baseman and the team needs a first baseman by the time you get to the top minors, you've got it made. If not, you rot—with apologies to Edgar Guest.

What I would like to do, though, is set down my impressions of minor league life and maybe clear up some of this phony glamour the drum beaters and their bosses have been spreading through the jungle, with an eye toward clueing in a kid as to exactly how tough it is. I hope I've been doing this. And rather than scaring a lot of kids out of the business, I hope to make them more determined to make it. It's probably the only business in the world where the fun you have is directly proportional to the work you do.

The thing is, baseball, while being a fantastic game and a beautiful sport (maybe someday we'll all understand the difference), is *not* played by heroes and gods. For every Stan Musial, there are a hundred Jose Pagans. For every Sandy Koufax, there are a hundred Roger Craigs.

The game is played by guys who started out as kids with acne, or college guys who got a big bonus but whose only talent rests in being able to beat other college teams. It's played by guys who have wives to support and kids to feed and who go to the movies and who have fights with their in-laws. They have financial problems, health problems and tax problems. They get warts, hiccups and hangovers, and are sometimes constipated—although walking the first man up in the ninth will usually cure this latter ailment.

I think the game would be better off if more kids understood what it takes to become a Biggie player. Talent, yes—but the same kind of talent it takes to become a good sword-swallower: lots of practice, but you get an awful lot of blisters in the process.

The glamour is great. I loved it. I loved the drama, too. I think I had more fun in those commando games with Dallas and Dick than I did in most of the games I pitched. Which tells you two things: 1) I usually didn't pitch very good games; 2) I like to play commandos.

It's quite a feeling, for instance, when a young kid becomes a hero and is asked to make personal appearances at a department store.

My first time was at Hipoint-Thomasville in '57, when they had a "Hi-Tom Day" and each player from the team would be at a store to sign autographs and talk to the kids.

The kids would turn out by the thousands, to adore the gods in uniforms. Some sample questions:

"Do you like to win?"

"Do you like to play ball?"

"Can I have your hat?"

"Why don't you be an outfielder?"

"What store is Freddie Hopke at?"

"Who the hell are you?"

It's really a terrible bore, no matter how much you like

kids. I guess every player all the way up to the Biggies gets a little bored by personal appearances and just puts in his two hours or so and gets out of the place.

In the minors, though, the townsfolk are usually good to the players. Aside from the clowns whose only purpose in life is to save their tip-money to buy a ticket so they can ride the players, the folks who like baseball and come out regularly to enjoy the game are really great to the team as a whole and to the players individually.

They'd have banquets and Kiwanis functions, etc., and they'd make a large fuss over the team. Mostly business-men and women. They'd even telephone the club, in the smaller minors, and let it be known that they had some space to board some of the single players.

Since you only came to town about three days before the season opened, the players didn't have much time to check out places to live or eat. There are workouts, pub-licity photos, night-and-day practice on the field to get used to conditions, and a thousand other things. A guy is very appreciative of a family who boards him and makes sure he gets fed decently. The hometown folks who boarded the players were doing a greater favor than they realized. Like keeping us sober most of the time.

The newspapers were good to the team, too. In a big city, if a manager or player makes a mistake, or a losing streak comes along, all the frustrated ballplayers who are running the sports sections ride hell out of the team in bitter tirades and indignant editorials. In the small towns the papers were always good to us and I think it helped win a few games. They'd always have the attitude that while nobody likes to lose, it does happen but by-God-we'll-pull-out-of-it-and-tear-up-the-league.

Which is a pretty healthy attitude. Look where it's getting the Mets.

Another good thing in favor of the ballplayers is girls. In fact, girls are good things in favor of anyone. If they put their mind to it.

After night games in the summer down in the minors, we'd go to a bar or some place to have a few beers before dinner. Well, before breakfast, anyway. We'd go to a place to have a few beers while picking up some girls, is what we did.

The funny thing is that the girls would come out to the ball park and watch the game, and then they'd know exactly which bars we hung out in and would go there. By the time we were showered and finished ribbing each other or giving Pete Cera a bad time, the gals would be all settled at the bars and we could just move right in.

We would always go to the country club with no special passes or anything, even though none of us were members and it was a private club. And as soon as the girls discovered we were hanging out at the country club, they'd all join up and be there when we walked in every night. Minor league towns are jam-packed with girls who somehow are wild about minor league ballplayers. Kind of like buying stock in a small company, I guess.

It was really funny. I've heard of these islands in some exotic area of the earth where men are at a premium and the women kill each other to get one, but I'm sure it's nothing like a ballplayer's life in a minor league town.

He's a god. The local boys hate to see the season start. They're all football fans.

But this is a baseball book, isn't it?

The girls' and the inhabitants' attitudes aren't the only difference, though, between major and minor league baseball. Playing conditions are infinitely better in the Biggies. Even in Candlestick Park. The difference is something like the difference between playing golf in Boca Raton and playing golf in a mine field. There are lots of surprises.

The majors travel by plane, for one thing, and the minors travel by bus, station wagon, or llama, if it's feasible—and cheap. Majors stay in big hotels with suites and charge accounts, and the minors stay in fleabags with one head for the whole team. Down the hall. I've seen guys have to sleep on cots or on the floor on minor league road trips.

The Biggie players have three or four uniforms for home and the same for the road. After the first game of a doubleheader, you go change into a clean suit. Freshly pressed and spotless uniforms, nice clean sweat socks, half a dozen jocks, the whole works. In the minors, though, you have one suit for home and one for the road. You play the second game of a doubleheader in the same stinking sweaty suit, and just hope nobody asks for your autograph.

Big leaguers have five or six bats, and the minor leaguers have one. If it breaks, you use someone else's until you buy another or else find a sturdy table leg somewhere. When the big leaguers are down in supply, they just order more. When the minor leaguers are down in supply, they take aspirin.

But equipment endorsements save the day. The only thing a club furnishes a player is his uniform and related apparel. The player pays for everything else: glove, shoes, slide pads, shorts, jocks—everything. It gets expensive, too.

A lot of times the tools, though, are supplied by some equipment firm. Most players on the way up are signed by firms such as Wilson, MacGregor, Spaulding, Rawlings, etc., and they then get all their gloves, shoes, and bats furnished them free of charge. I signed with MacGregor, which I think is one of the best sporting goods firms in the business.

I heard a lot about guys having trouble with some firms they signed with—not getting their equipment fast enough, or some other gripes—but I never had a single complaint with MacGregor. They signed me in '58, since at that time I looked like I was going to go all the way up. (When a player makes it, he endorses the firm's equipment, so that if I'd made it, we'd now be able to buy a Jerry Kettle glove. You can still buy one, actually; it's a Robin Roberts model and I'm selling it for only $10.)

MacGregor was great. They'd send me a catalog every season, and I could order anything I wanted out of it. Major league pitchers use a leather patch on the toe of their pivot shoe, instead of the metal plate seen on high school equipment. Every time I ordered shoes, MacGregor would send them to me with the patch already sewed on. Whenever I ordered a glove—a Robin Roberts model—I'd get exactly what I wanted and I'd get it almost immediately.

The contract you sign with them is just a piece of paper saying you won't sign with another firm and that MacGregor will have a claim on you when you're a star. Usually, they'll put some proviso in to the effect that when you're a major leaguer, you'll get so much free stuff every year, say $500 worth. It's generally a good deal, and most players in the Biggies have such contracts.

I also signed with Topp's Bubble Gum. This, again, is so that when I became a big star they could put my picture on a card so kids could trade one Jerry Kettle for five Sandy Koufaxes (laugh it up, folks!). Topp's promised their players a selection of almost anything in a very large catalog they had—as soon as the player made the majors. Mack Burke, who played a year with the Phillies, picked out a beautiful stereo set worth about a grand. Beautiful thing.

So that's another thing I lost out on.

The funniest thing I've ever seen in this regard is when Richie Ashburn was making a Camel ad for television. We were down at Jack Russell Stadium in Clearwater, and Richie was giving the television crew fits because he'd never smoked in his life and the smoke would get into his eyes, or else he'd start coughing, or look like a tweak when he held the thing. They had to do about half a dozen takes to get old Richie looking just right with a Camel.

He hasn't smoked since, either.

*   *   *

The biggest difference, I'd say, is actually the playing conditions. The majors have ground crews continually manicuring the field, making it perfect for playing. The parks have great lighting, the dugouts are beautiful and well-supplied—looking like mobile homes—and the clubhouse itself often looks as if it had been designed by Hugh Hefner.

I've played in minor league parks where we'd have maybe 60 lights lighting the whole goddam field. Less lighting, say, than you probably have on your back porch. Certainly less lights than there are in a single light standard in a major league park. In fact, the other night I was changing a flat tire on the San Bernardino Freeway at eleven o'clock, and when I lit a flare to put a few hundred feet behind my car, I could have sworn I heard someone call out, "Ball one!"

If you don't think *lights* make a difference! If a kid trying to work his way up can't see the ball, he's not going to look forward to playing. If a minor league batting average is, say, .300, it's a pretty good bet he's a much better hitter and would have a better average under conditions where he at least knew approximately when the pitcher wound up.

When an infield looks like Hiroshima, and bad hops are being called against you, it can reverse your whole year and sadly affect your record. Pitching a close game, going down to the wire for that win, and a bad hop or an outfielder losing the ball in the darkness sending in the winning run against you—that all still adds up to another big fat digit in your lost column.

Of course, the other teams play under the same conditions, but the mistake everyone makes is that just because everyone has the same handicap doesn't mean good baseball is being played or a guy is showing his real timbre as a ballplayer. If you held a track meet on an iceberg, would you be able to tell who were the best runners?

I sincerely believe that better minor leaguer playing conditions and, in some cases, better living conditions, would help a parent club get better ballplayers out of its talent. You could make a lot more good decisions when you know a kid has had all the advantages before you decide to send him up or down. As it is now, a club may think a kid's having a bad year when, in fact, a good lawn mower would add three games to his win column.

In my own case, I've played in ball parks where the mounds weren't even regulation. One time we measured one and instead of 60 feet, 6 inches away from the plate, this thing was 61 feet away. Another time, in Mattoon, we measured it and the mound turned out to be 59 feet, 6 inches away from home—an entire foot closer! And they're supposed to be checking all this stuff. Twelve inches means a helluva lot to a slider or a curve, and makes a fast ball seem like a ballistic missile. It seriously hinders a pitcher's performance if it's long, and hinders the batter if it's short.

I've also played in one ball park where the right field fence was 205 feet away from the plate. 205 feet! A *bunt* would go all the way! I pitched to one guy and jammed him on the wrists, but he swung anyway, broke his bat clean in half, and the goddam ball was a home run. Yet in the game write-up, "Home Run Off Kettle" is all that showed up. Sometimes when Harris was throwing to second on a steal, I'd pray he wouldn't overthrow into the center field bleachers.

I strongly suggest the major leagues use some of that bonus money they're throwing around to inspect seriously the playing conditions in their farm systems. Might be worth the time and dough, especially if they discover Joe Doakes hits fifty percentage points higher when all the mounds are regulation, or Clyde Fink would only give up half as many home runs if there were grass between the infield and the fences.

If there *were* an infield, that is.

The conditions probably make it tougher on the bonus babies more than anyone. We all play ragged baseball, but the bonus babies are supposed to do everything right. The money's probably worth it, whether you make it or not, but being a bonus baby is a tough life.

They're teammates, so naturally there isn't much resentment or serious riding, but there's a lot of good-natured kidding. I guess it's good training. Mack Burke was a $40,000 bonus baby, which at that time was equivalent to the $100,000 handouts they're giving out now. Mack would really get ridden by the gang when he blew one, but even when he was going strong he'd usually get a few good jabs. My favorite was to bug him about buying the team a new set of uniforms. Whenever a patch would come off or a rip would appear after a game, I'd go over to Mack's locker and announce to everyone that he was going to use some of his forty grand to get us some new uniforms. He'd laugh with the rest of us, but I often wondered whether bonus babies don't feel an extra little something in the way of determination—responsibility, I guess—to show they're worth their bonuses.

Sometimes, though, when a bonus baby blew one and things weren't going just right in the first place, and maybe you were feeling down in the dumps anyway, you'd come up with a sterling remark like "Holy Cripes, forty grand for *that?*" This always made the bonus baby feel bad, all right, but more often than not it made the player who said it feel a lot worse when he came out of his bad mood and realized what he'd said. You always look for something to blame, and a bonus baby was a built-in target for the jibes of the poorer players. Maybe they should have teams composed only of bonus babies.

There's one true test of a guy's ballplaying maturity. The bonus baby who's in the Biggies doesn't give a damn about getting razzed. In the first place, it's part of the game, and in the second place he can't go any higher and he's pulling down a good salary plus his high bonus so the hell with the crowd. The other guys, guys like Mack, say, who are playing A ball and have a long way to go, need somebody to pull for them. There's always the razzing about his bonus, and the guy can get pretty discouraged. But a mature ballplayer will never seriously ride him and instead will give him a lift whenever he can. After a particularly bad day, a lot of us would cheer Mack up with some comment or other.

When you see a no-bonus guy sit down next to a bonus

baby who just lost a game and say, "What the hell, buddy, we all kick one once in a while," you know you've at least one classy ballplayer on your team. We had a helluva lot of classy ballplayers in A ball.

Hell, even the umpires have their troubles. Umpires in the minors are the same as the ballplayers: they're breaking in and trying to make it to the Biggies.

Naturally, not being experienced, a young umpire in the minor leagues will make a lot of mistakes, a lot of pretty bad calls. It's the same old story of confidence, really. The Biggie umps are confident as hell and call the games the way they want. They're the bosses and they know it; they take charge, relax, and don't let anything bother them. The minor league umps don't have this trait yet, and so they'll often be indecisive, unsure of whether they should change their minds and switch a call. It's one thing to learn adamancy in umpire school, but when you call a very close play and an entire team of young idiots charges you, you start to wonder about maybe being wrong. And when you switch a call, you get into trouble because then the young bunch of idiots in the *gray* uniforms start to charge you.

If a minor league ump makes a call and one team jumps all over him, his fear will be obvious. And because it's obvious, the team rants and raves all the harder. If he does reverse a decision, they crucify him. When he admits he's wrong he gets something like "What the hell kind of umpire are you?" from the players and he usually winds up sort of shaken.

In one game against Binghamton—it was the tenth in-

ning, 2–2—we had the bases loaded. John Herrnstein was
on third, with one out, and Ted Savage was hitting. I had
been pitching and wanted to win pretty badly, praying
for Ted to knock in Herrnstein.

Ted tapped a weak one to the right of the mound and
Herrnstein, a real moose, started churning for the plate.
The pitcher flipped the ball to his catcher for the force-
out, and Herrnstein slid. The catcher—we thought—had
his foot on the plate for the out, but the ump waved a
big "Safe" sign.

He forgot the bases were loaded. (The ump, by the way,
was Tom Ravashiere, who's in Triple-A ball now and
a great guy.)

Anyway, we stifled our laughs and grabbed our jackets
fast and headed for the clubhouse. Charlie Silvera, the
Binghamton manager at the time, came storming out like
a wild man and he and about ten other players jumped all
over Ravashiere. Before it was all over, Ravashiere had
remembered the play was a force-out and explained to
Silvera, as his way out of it, that that catcher had missed
the plate.

We found out later on that Ravashiere at first tried to
tell Silvera that his catcher hadn't *tagged* Herrnstein,
which of course made Silvera turn blue. But Ravashiere
got out of it with his catcher's-foot story. It was a win in
my pocket, so I couldn't say anything, but Tommy really
blew that one. I thought Silvera would lose his eyeballs
with rage.

Another time, in Little Rock, Dave Nicholson was on
third base and someone hit a fly ball to the outfield. Dick

Teed, our veteran, was catching, and whoever threw the ball to the plate threw a perfect strike. Teed had Nicholson by ten feet.

Teed caught the ball and braced himself for the collision. When Nicholson hit Teed, he rammed the ball and glove right into Teed's chest, knocking Teed back a few feet, but Teed still held on to it. Nicholson knew he was out and was running back to the dugout mad as hell at himself when the ump yelled "Safe!"

Lucchesi was a madman. Just about everyone on our bench had taken turns screaming and ranting at the ump when Lucchesi went on a sit-down strike on home plate. He said he was going to stay there until the ump reversed his decision, explaining that Teed hadn't tagged Nicholson but Nicholson had rammed the ball and glove right up against Teed and so, in effect, had tagged himself. He *had* to be tagged!

So the ump threw out Lucchesi and Teed and a few others, me included. It was the only time I'd ever been thrown out of a game. I had sailed onto the field, one by one, every batting helmet we had and the ump finally cleared out the whole bench. When the furor was over, the ump had to come into the clubhouse and ask us to send out a pitcher—there were only eight guys left on our side!

The umps have the same authority as they do in the majors. They can clear a bench or throw out a manager or player or fine someone. Because of this, and the fact there's an automatic $10 fine for getting thrown out, it's a good idea to avoid arguments. And the best way to keep

on an ump's good side, even if you are in an argument, is
not to show him up in front of a crowd.

In other words, if a ball's outside but it's called a strike,
you can say almost everything in the book to the ump as
long as you make it look like you're asking him how he
enjoyed his lunch. Once you start ranting at him and
waving your arms and making overly emphatic gestures,
you've got $10 less for beer money. You can turn around
and tap your spikes or back out a bit, all the while looking at center field and telling the ump about his ancestors,
but if you turn around and yell at him he looks bad to
the crowd and he'll throw you out. One time Dick Harris
got thrown out just for turning around and looking at the
ump—he didn't say a word!

Umpires don't like to be shown up. They don't like a
player to make them look bad, no matter who's right or
who's wrong. For instance, you never charge the plate
from the mound when you're upset at a call. If you do,
keep on going to the showers, because you're going to get
the thumb.

From the mound, a pitcher often walks down four or
five steps to yell something, but if he comes all the way in
he's had it. The usual saying is, "Goddam it, Joe, bear
down back there!" Or else, "Ball?! C'mon, for crissake,
start bearing down, Ump, huh?"

But you don't charge the plate and you don't show up
the ump. If you do, you get the thumb and you have to
find out about the rest of the game while wishing everyone used Dial.

*   *   *

Superstitions are fun, too. They're probably more prevalent in the minors than in the Biggies, because the guys seem to believe more in luck. Maybe that's because they need more of it under the conditions they're playing.

I guess the guy in the Biggies figures he made it on his own merit—because he has made it—but the guys in the minors think every little thing that happens might be a good omen or a lucky charm that will rocket them to stardom.

Lucchesi was the most superstitious guy I ever met. In Chattanooga, we won a string of games in a row and Frank looked like Attila the Hun because he wouldn't get a haircut while we were winning. Something about the last time he got one, we lost the game. Maybe he was right, who knows? We won 13 out of 15 games while Frank looked like Moses.

Frank wouldn't step on any base lines, either, a superstition that's practiced on a large scale in the Biggies. Frank would hop around the field like a rabbit whenever he was arguing with an ump in the vicinity of home plate, where there are lots of base lines. Half the time we'd listen for bagpipes just to check our own sanity.

Frank would put his right shoe on first, and both shoes before his pants. One time we were playing at Winston-Salem and my name showed up as *Gettle*. This was because Frank had made a mistake in the lineup card the last time I'd pitched, spelling my name *Gettle*, and I had won. So I was *Gettle* again, to Frank, and he put it down that way on the card. Consequently, when I went out to the mound, the official scorer came down to the dugout and told Lucchesi I couldn't play because I wasn't on the roster. The umpires agreed, and it was quite a while before anyone would believe that Lucchesi put the wrong name down on purpose and that I was really *K*ettle.

Anyway, I won the game and when I sent home the clipping to my folks the box score said some guy named Gettle had won the game. In fact, Frank still wanted the official scorer to put my name down as Gettle, even after he'd convinced everyone that I was really Kettle.

I never had any real hot superstitions myself, aside from the normal ones pitchers have. I never stepped on a base line when I was coming on or going off the field. Some first basemen always run directly to the bag and step on it or kick it before they're ready to start the inning, and some outfielders will tag a certain bag on their way out to the field and when they're coming in. A lot of these are just habits, though.

Every time Tony Curry batted, he'd hit his bat on the plate, take a few practice swings, and then wait with the bat on his shoulders the way many guys do. Only Tony, when he was doing this, would reach down and grab his crotch to hitch up his pants. I don't know what this did to the girls in the stands, but we'd laugh like crazy whenever Tony was up. It used to bug Lucchesi to death.

The funny thing was that Tony never did it before any subsequent pitch, only that first time he stepped into the box.

Yeah, it's great fun and a big thrill. If you're a single guy. Married guys who have to worry about supporting a family never enjoy it as much—what there is to enjoy, I mean. No matter how much they love the game, the living is crummy, the pay is crummy and the playing conditions are crummy. More often than not, your salary is the crummiest of all.

Barring any brilliant trades such as the one where the Pirates gave away Dick Groat, Dick Stewart and their chances for a pennant for the next five years, the Phillies should take all the marbles in 1965, if they don't choke. That makes fifteen years since they won a pennant, assuming they'll win in '65. Isn't that the time it's supposed to take for a whole mess of monkeys with a whole mess of typewriters to write a whole mess of encyclopedias? By God, the Mets have a chance yet!

The Phillies gave me a lot, really. I have memories and still some loot in a savings account and the biggest scrapbook you'll ever see, one which I seriously plan to use to brighten the eyes of my sons and grandchildren. I love the Phillies, and I'm rooting for them to win the flag *one* of these years. Soon, like. So I want to talk about the Phillies.

The Phillies' keeping on the same old guys instead of building up their young players contributed a lot to their downfall in the Fifties. In '56, when I was asked to stay over and train with the Phils, they still had Stan Lopata, Del Ennis, Richie Ashburn, Granny Hamner, Willie "Puddinhead" Jones and some others who were on their way down (Robin Roberts and Curt Simmons were still great, though). And this was seven years after the Whiz Kids won a pennant in '50. The Phillies were still hoping they could win again with the same team—seven years later. It's only since they've brought up new blood and started giving the young guys a chance that they've become a contender again.

You have to spend money to win a pennant. The Yankees dominate that other league over there because they have a fantastic farm organization and bring up their own boys. How many times do you see the Yankees—or the Dodgers, for that matter—buy a player from another team? Meanwhile, though, the other clubs in the American League are pinching pennies and trying to use rockets and fireworks to win a pennant. It can't be done. Those gimmicks and tricks are all right, because they may bring in some extra gate money, but the best way to bring in dough is to have a winning team. And the only way to have a winning team is to field nine good ballplayers. Washington, Kansas City and those teams are most likely the penny-pinchingest teams in the league. And as long as they hold those pursestrings real tight, they'll have to continue relying on their fireworks and movable fences and "pennant porches." Because they'll never see the first division. Hell, if Wrigley would break down and buy some lights for night baseball, his club would probably double its income. Imagine a guy like Ernie Banks never being in a World Series. Ted Williams was in only one. And what Robin Roberts could have done with a winning team would take a book in itself!

I think if you examine each of the top teams around, you'll find almost without exception they're the teams that have extensive farm systems and aren't afraid to

spend money to cultivate a good ballplayer. Don't castigate the Yanks for dominating the league; castigate the
other seven or so teams who aren't doing a thing to better
their situation. Look how the Angels' Gene Autry and
Bob Reynolds spent the dough when they got the club
a few years back. The Angels can now give the Yanks fits,
and a while back played some pretty good ball. Spend
money, win a pennant. Simple, eh?

So the Phillies started buying guys like Gene Freese
and Wally Post, but they still were the older guys who
weren't helping the club any. The Phils found themselves
in the same old rut, and they didn't have anyone to bring
up from their own farm system. That's when they started
the rookie school, which was a year or so before I signed.
Then they started giving guys a chance, instead of pinching pennies and cutting corners—guys like Dallas Green,
Art Mahaffey and Bobby Wine, or, more recently, guys
like Richie Allen and John Herrnstein.

And so, as the sun sets on the horizon and Camp Clearwater, the Phillies have a fabulous chance to win this
year's pennant.

Ex-minor league players, by the way, even while the
chances are greatest that they don't have any extensive
higher education, usually have good jobs to come home
to. Now, I'm working in my father's nursery and my
brother and I will probably take it over when he retires,
or when we stage a bloodless coup. Dick Harris is a
teacher. Gordy Figard sells trailers for his dad's business.

To indicate what a minor league ballplayer does when

he finds out he isn't going to make it—by word of mouth, usually—take a look at the following column. It's by Ray Keyes, from his "Sun-Spots" column in the Williamsport *Sun-Gazette* of September 9, 1958. It gives you some idea of what the players do when they aren't playing.

During the off-season the cast of the Williamsport Grays is engaged in quite a variety of occupations, but for eight the winter means hitting the books instead of baseballs. Some of the boys are furthering their college education.

Here are their early September plans for the fast approaching off-season.

Manager Dick Carter, after a vacation at the shore, will resume his sales-public relations work with a Philadelphia brewing distributor.

Bob Milo, halfway through his junior year at Wayne State University, will return there to pursue his studies in the advertising field. In his early college days he studied journalism. College is at home, for Bob resides in Detroit.

Mack Burke, after a 15-day period of Army drilling, plans to return to the University of Texas. He's from Houston.

Wilbur Johnson will continue working for his master's degree in civil engineering at the University of Colorado.

Sales work for a Chicago corporation in his native New York City is on the agenda for Joe Gaskin.

Back in Newark, N.J., Fred Hopke in past winters has been a tool and die maker. But not this time; he seeks different employment.

Dale Bennetch, a sophomore at Millersburg State

Tchrs. College, will miss the books this year. He's slated for six-months of Army duty. Dale is from Newmanstown.

In the past, Earl Hunsinger has sold insurance in Winfield, Ala., but this year he hopes to play winter ball.

Bob Frederick, of Philadelphia suburb Cheltenham, has sold autos and worked in a refinery, but now is looking for other employment here in Williamsport.

Jerry Kettle does landscaping work in Pasadena, Cal., for the nursery firm owned by his father.

Bob Hunt is another collegian. The Birmingham lad will resume his business administration study at the University of Alabama. He's a senior.

For Bib Gill the winter means working in a produce co-op in Montrose, Colo.

And Marco Mainini, now that he calls Schenectady his home, has employment in a restaurant there.

Art Hirst is a construction worker for his father out of Atco, N.J. Last winter he worked in the Hazleton area.

Nineteen-year-old Ed Keegan, new in the employment and baseball world, has a promise of a job at a Camden, N.J., newspaper.

Fred Van Dusen's plan is to play winter ball, and Karl Heron is certain to perform again in the Panama winter circuit. Van Dusen, from New York City, says he's not sure where he'll play.

Princetonian John Easton, of Trenton, N.J., with the degree in electrical engineering, has no difficulty finding work in his profession.

Anyone need a shrub or two?

Oh, well. It's fun looking back like this. I'm at the end of my scrapbook and all that's left is black pages, which I hope isn't an omen, and some scraps.

Here's a Chattanooga team picture. Johnny Herrnstein is in it, and Milo and Lee Elia. So's John Boozer and Dick Teed. But who the hell is Jerry Kettle? And here are about fifteen copies of the story and photos of the game that Ted Savage won for me. Good old Ted. Helluva guy.

And a photo of Monrovia-Duarte High School, when I was in my prime. Apparently, anyway. And a picture of Barney Glenn, who managed the Monrovia Merchants where I played for so long.

Which reminds me. There'll be a Kettle yet in the Biggies. My brother Stevie, who's now seventeen and who'll be bigger than me when he's full grown, recently was out at the park watching a game between the Merchants and some other team. Barney knew him, of course, and was shy a man—which often happened and we'd usually play some kid just to fill out the field and give the kid a large-sized thrill—so Steve played a few innings. A few weeks later, Barney let Stevie pitch for five innings.

This baby brother of mine struck out seven men and won the game. I guess he inherited his older brother's cockiness, though, because he strode off that mound like he owned the world. That night at dinner he told me he wanted to become a major league pitcher and I almost choked to death on my Pablum.

The kid's serious. He's also pretty good. Just like I was.

So he'll play there a while in Monrovia, go to Pasadena College and play ball, and some scout will sign him up. Only he'll get about $30,000 for a bonus. Except his big brother will jump him some night as he comes in and claim half the loot. After all, I'm beating my brains out to teach him something about the game, aren't I?

So just last week the kid's sliding into third base somewhere and broke his leg. And from the way it sounds outside this evening, it sure as hell seems like a hurricane's brewing up. Hope Stevie doesn't hear it.

Helluva way to start a career.